Modern JavaScript Guide

Your Step-by-Step Guide to Modern Code

Pedro Middysunn

Contents

1
Meeting JavaScript

Get ready to step into the dynamic world of web development. This chapter introduces you to JavaScript, the language that breathes life into websites. We are going to explore what it is, trace its origins, and understand why it has become such a cornerstone of modern technology. Think of this as your initial handshake with JavaScript – we'll cover the basics and ensure you have the simple tools needed to start experimenting right away. By the end of this chapter, you'll have written your very first lines of code and be prepared to dive deeper into its core concepts.

What Exactly Is JavaScript?

At its heart, JavaScript is a **programming language** primarily used to create interactive and dynamic content on websites. Imagine a website as a house. HTML (Hyper-Text Markup Language) would be the structural framework – the walls, floors, and roof. CSS (Cascading Style Sheets) would be the paint, wallpaper, and furniture – defining the visual appearance and layout. JavaScript, then, is the electricity, plumbing, and automation – it makes things *happen*.

Without JavaScript, webpages are mostly static displays of information, like a printed brochure. With JavaScript, you can:

- Make elements appear, disappear, or animate.
- Validate user input in forms before sending it.
- Fetch new data from a server without reloading the page.

- Create sliders, carousels, and interactive maps.
- Build complex web applications, including games.

It's a versatile, text-based language that runs directly in your web browser (and other places, as we'll see). You don't need special compilers or complex setup to get started with basic browser-based JavaScript.

A Brief History: From Netscape to Now

JavaScript's story begins in the mid-1990s, during the early days of the web. Netscape Communications, creators of the popular Netscape Navigator browser, recognized the need for a simple scripting language to make web pages more interactive. HTML was great for structure, but it couldn't *do* much.

In 1995, a programmer named **Brendan Eich** was tasked with creating this language. Legend has it, he developed the first prototype in just 10 days! Initially, it was called Mocha, then LiveScript, and finally, in a marketing move to align it with the popular Java language (though they are **very different** languages), it became JavaScript.

Microsoft soon released its own version, JScript, for Internet Explorer. This led to compatibility issues – code written for one browser might not work in the other. To solve this, JavaScript was submitted to ECMA International, an organization that creates standards. In 1997, they released the first official standard for the language, called **ECMAScript** (often abbreviated as ES).

Since then, ECMAScript has evolved through numerous versions (ES3, ES5, ES6/ES2015, ES2016, and so on), adding new features and capabilities. Modern JavaScript, which this book focuses on, incorporates these powerful additions that make writing complex applications much easier. While "JavaScript" is the common name, "ECMAScript" refers to the official specification. Think of ECMAScript as the rulebook and JavaScript as the most popular implementation of those rules.

Why Learn JavaScript Today?

Learning JavaScript is one of the most valuable investments you can make if you're interested in technology. Why?

1. **Ubiquity:** It runs on virtually every web browser across desktops, tablets, and smartphones. You don't need users to install anything extra.
2. **Versatility:** Originally confined to browsers, JavaScript has exploded! With environments like Node.js (which we'll touch on later), you can use JavaScript

to build server-side applications, mobile apps, desktop software, and even control hardware.

3. **Huge Community:** JavaScript has one of the largest and most active developer communities in the world. This means abundant resources, tutorials, libraries, frameworks, and readily available help when you get stuck.

4. **Career Opportunities:** JavaScript developers are in extremely high demand across various industries. Whether it's front-end development (user interfaces), back-end development (server logic), or full-stack (both), JavaScript skills open countless doors.

5. **It's Engaging:** Making things happen visually on a webpage provides immediate feedback, which can be incredibly rewarding and motivating for learners.

JavaScript Everywhere: Browsers and Beyond

As mentioned, JavaScript's reach extends far beyond making buttons change color in a browser.

- **Front-End Web Development:** This is its traditional home. Libraries and frameworks like React, Angular, Vue, and Svelte are built with JavaScript and power many of the complex web applications you use daily.
- **Back-End Web Development: Node.js** allows developers to run JavaScript on servers. This means you can use the same language for both the client-side (browser) and server-side logic of a web application, simplifying the development process.
- **Mobile App Development:** Frameworks like React Native, NativeScript, and Ionic allow you to build native-like mobile apps for iOS and Android using JavaScript.
- **Desktop Applications:** Tools such as Electron (which powers applications like VS Code, Slack, and Discord) enable the creation of cross-platform desktop applications using JavaScript, HTML, and CSS.
- **Game Development:** Numerous libraries and engines (like Phaser or Babylon.js) facilitate game development for the web and other platforms using JavaScript.
- **Internet of Things (IoT):** JavaScript can even be used to program microcontrollers and interact with hardware devices.

While this book primarily focuses on the fundamentals and browser-based applications, understanding this wider context shows the immense power and potential of the language you are about to learn.

Setting Up Your Playground

The fantastic thing about starting with JavaScript is that you likely already have the necessary tools! You don't need to install complex software right away.

Using Your Browser's Developer Console

Every modern web browser includes a set of built-in tools for web developers, often called "Developer Tools" or "DevTools". One of the most important parts is the **Console**. The console allows you to type and execute JavaScript commands directly, view messages logged from scripts, and inspect errors.

How to Open the Console:

- **Google Chrome:** Press F12, or right-click on a webpage, select "Inspect", and then click the "Console" tab. (On macOS: Option + Command + J)
- **Mozilla Firefox:** Press F12, or right-click on a webpage, select "Inspect Element", and then click the "Console" tab. (On macOS: Option + Command + K)
- **Microsoft Edge:** Press F12, or right-click on a webpage, select "Inspect", and then click the "Console" tab.
- **Safari:** You might need to enable the Develop menu first (Preferences > Advanced > Show Develop menu in menu bar). Then, press Option + Command + C or go to Develop > Show JavaScript Console.

Once the console is open, you'll see a prompt, usually marked with a > symbol. Try typing this command and pressing Enter:

```
console.log("Hello from the Console!");
```

You should see the text "Hello from the Console!" printed on the next line.

```
> console.log("Hello from the Console!");
Hello from the Console!
undefined
```

(Don't worry about the undefined *that might appear after your output for now; it's the return value of* console.log, *which we'll discuss later.)*

The console is excellent for quick tests, experimenting with small snippets of code, and debugging.

Choosing a Code Editor

While the console is great for simple commands, you'll write larger programs in separate files. You *could* use a basic text editor like Notepad (Windows) or TextEdit (Mac), but a dedicated **code editor** will make your life much easier.

Code editors offer features specifically designed for programming, such as:

- **Syntax Highlighting:** Makes code easier to read by coloring different parts (keywords, variables, strings).
- **Auto-Completion:** Suggests code as you type, saving time and reducing typos.
- **Error Highlighting:** Points out potential syntax errors before you even run the code.
- **File Management:** Helps organize projects with multiple files.
- **Integrated Terminals:** Many allow you to run commands directly within the editor.

Popular free code editors include:

- **Visual Studio Code (VS Code):** Extremely popular, feature-rich, and extensible. A great choice for beginners and professionals alike.
- **Sublime Text:** Lightweight, fast, and highly customizable.
- **Atom:** Another open-source editor developed by GitHub.

Download and install one of these. We recommend **VS Code** for its excellent JavaScript support out of the box. Spend a little time exploring its interface.

Running JavaScript with Node.js (A Quick Look)

As we discussed, JavaScript isn't limited to the browser. **Node.js** is a runtime environment that allows you to execute JavaScript code *outside* of a web browser, typically on a server or your local machine.

Do you need Node.js right now? No. For the initial chapters focusing on browser interaction (DOM manipulation, events), you only need a browser and a code editor.

However, Node.js is essential for server-side development and often used for tooling (like running build processes or installing project dependencies) in modern front-end workflows. We'll explore Node.js in more detail much later in the book (Chapter 19), but it's good to know it exists.

If you *are* curious, you can download and install it from the official Node.js website. Installation usually includes **npm** (Node Package Manager), a tool for managing reusable code packages, which is also fundamental to the modern JavaScript ecosystem. Once installed, you could save a JavaScript file (e.g., `hello.js`) and run it from your computer's terminal like this:

```
node hello.js
```

Again, **this is optional for now**. Stick with the browser console and code editor for the upcoming chapters.

Your First JavaScript Code

Let's move beyond the console and write code in a file, the way you'll build real applications.

1. **Create a Project Folder:** Make a new folder on your computer named something like `js-basics`.

2. **Create HTML File:** Inside `js-basics`, use your code editor to create a new file named `index.html`. Paste the following basic HTML structure into it:

```html
<!DOCTYPE html>
<html lang="en">
<head>
    <meta charset="UTF-8">
    <meta name="viewport" content="width=device-width, initial-
scale=1.0">
    <title>My First JavaScript Page</title>
</head>
<body>
    <h1>Learning JavaScript!</h1>

    <!-- The magic happens here -->
    <script src="app.js"></script>
</body>
</html>
```

- `<!DOCTYPE html>`: Declares the document type.
- `<html>`: The root element.
- `<head>`: Contains meta-information (character set, viewport settings, title). The browser reads this, but it's not directly displayed.
- `<body>`: Contains the visible page content (headings, paragraphs, images, and our script!).

- `<script src="app.js"></script>`: This is the crucial tag. It tells the browser to fetch and execute the JavaScript code found in the file named `app.js`. We place it just before the closing `</body>` tag. This is common practice because it ensures the HTML elements (like the `<h1>`) exist *before* the script tries to interact with them.

3. **Create JavaScript File:** In the *same* `js-basics` folder, create another file named `app.js`. This is where your JavaScript code will live.

4. **Write JavaScript:** Add the following line to `app.js`:

```
console.log("Hello from the app.js file!");

// You can add more commands here later
```

- `console.log()` is a built-in function used to display messages in the browser's developer console. It's incredibly useful for checking values and understanding what your code is doing.

5. **Open the HTML File:** Find the `index.html` file in your computer's file explorer and double-click it. It should open in your default web browser.

6. **Check the Console:** You'll see the "Learning JavaScript!" heading on the page. Now, open the browser's developer console (using `F12` or the methods described earlier). You should see the message:

```
Hello from the app.js file!
```

You've successfully linked and executed your first external JavaScript file. You've taken your first real step into programming with JavaScript.

Chapter Summary

This chapter gave you a bird's-eye view of JavaScript: what it is, its history, why it's relevant, and the basic tools you need. We explored the browser console for quick tests and set up a minimal HTML and JavaScript file structure, writing and running our very first command. You've seen that JavaScript is the engine that drives interactivity on the web and beyond.

Now that you're acquainted with JavaScript and have your environment set up, we're ready to dig into the core components of the language itself. In the next chapter, we'll explore the fundamental building blocks: how JavaScript represents different types of information (values and data types), how we store that information using labels (variables), and how to leave explanatory notes within our code (comments).

2

The Building Blocks

In the previous chapter, we got acquainted with JavaScript, understood its purpose, and set up our coding environment. Now, it's time to roll up our sleeves and start learning the language's fundamental grammar and vocabulary. Just like learning any spoken language requires understanding nouns, verbs, and sentence structure, learning JavaScript involves grasping its core components: how it represents information, how we label and store that information, and how we can leave notes within our code. This chapter lays the groundwork for everything that follows, introducing you to statements, comments, variables, and the basic data types that form the foundation of every JavaScript program.

JavaScript Statements

Think of a JavaScript program as a series of instructions given to the computer, much like a recipe provides steps to bake a cake. Each individual instruction or step in JavaScript is called a **statement**. Statements tell the computer to perform a specific action.

Consider the code we wrote in the last chapter:

```
console.log("Hello from the app.js file!");
```

This entire line is a single JavaScript statement. Its action is to log a message to the console. Most statements in JavaScript end with a semicolon (;). While JavaScript has rules for automatically inserting semicolons in some cases (a feature called Automatic Semicolon Insertion or ASI), it's generally considered good practice, especially for beginners, to **explicitly end each statement with a semicolon**. This makes your code clearer and prevents potential ambiguities.

You can have multiple statements, typically written on separate lines for readability:

```
console.log("First instruction.");
console.log("Second instruction.");
// *This code logs two separate messages to the console.*
```

Talking to Ourselves

As your programs become more complex, you'll find it helpful to leave notes within your code. These notes, called **comments**, are ignored by the JavaScript engine; they exist purely for human readers (including your future self!). Comments help explain *why* you wrote a piece of code a certain way, clarify complex logic, or temporarily disable lines of code without deleting them.

JavaScript provides two main ways to write comments:

Single-Line Comments

A single-line comment starts with two forward slashes (//) and continues to the end of that line. Anything after the // on that line is ignored.

```
// *This whole line is a comment.*

console.log("Hello!"); // *This comment explains the code.*

// console.log("This line is commented out, it won't run.");
```

Multi-Line Comments

For longer explanations or commenting out multiple lines at once, you can use multi-line comments. These start with /* and end with */. Everything between these markers is treated as a comment.

```
/*
   This is a multi-line comment.
   It can span several lines and is useful
   for more detailed explanations or temporarily
   disabling a larger block of code.
*/

console.log("This code will run.");

/*
console.log("This line won't run.");
console.log("Neither will this one.");
*/

console.log("This code will also run.");
```

Use comments wisely. Don't over-comment obvious code, but do explain the reasoning behind complex or potentially confusing parts. Good comments make your code much easier to understand and maintain.

Storing Information

Imagine you're organizing your pantry. You don't just pile everything randomly; you put items into containers (jars, boxes, bags) and maybe even label those containers ("Flour", "Sugar", "Coffee Beans"). Variables in JavaScript serve a similar purpose: they are **named containers for storing data values**. Instead of writing the same value repeatedly, you can store it in a variable and refer to it by its name.

Why use variables?

- **Reusability:** Store a value once and use it multiple times.
- **Readability:** Give descriptive names to data (e.g., `userName` instead of just `"Alice"`).
- **Maintainability:** If a value needs to change, you only need to update it in one place (where the variable is defined).

Declaring Variables

Before you can use a variable, you need to *declare* it, essentially creating the labeled container. JavaScript provides three keywords for declaring variables: `let`, `const`, and `var`.

1. `let`: Introduced in modern JavaScript (ES6), `let` allows you to declare variables whose values **can be reassigned** later. Variables declared with `let` are also **block-scoped**, meaning they are typically only accessible within the block of code (like inside an `if` statement or a loop, denoted by curly braces {}) where they are defined. We'll explore scope in detail in Chapter 9.

```
let message; // *Declare a variable named 'message'*
message = "Hello, JavaScript learners!"; // *Assign a value*
console.log(message); // *Output: Hello, JavaScript learners!*

message = "Time to learn variables!"; // *Reassign a new value*
console.log(message); // *Output: Time to learn variables!*

let userCount = 10; // *Declare and assign in one step*
userCount = userCount + 1; // *Increase the count*
console.log(userCount); // *Output: 11*
```

2. `const`: Also introduced in ES6, `const` is used to declare variables whose values **cannot be reassigned** after they are initially set. These are often called "constants". Like `let`, const variables are **block-scoped**. You **must** assign a value when you declare a const variable.

```
const birthYear = 1995; // *Declare and assign a constant*
console.log(birthYear); // *Output: 1995*

// *The following line would cause an error:*
// birthYear = 1996; // *TypeError: Assignment to constant variable.*

// *You must initialize a const:*
// const apiKey; // *SyntaxError: Missing initializer in const
declaration.*
```

Important Note: const doesn't make the *value itself* unchangeable, especially for objects and arrays (which we'll see in Chapters 6 and 7). It just prevents the variable from being reassigned to point to a *different* value.

3. `var`: This was the original way to declare variables in JavaScript before ES6. Variables declared with var have **function scope** or **global scope** (again, more on scope in Chapter 9) and **can be reassigned**. However, var has some quirks related to hoisting (covered in Chapter 9) and scope that can lead to confusion and bugs.

```
var score = 100;
score = 150; // *Reassignment is allowed*
console.log(score); // *Output: 150*
```

Recommendation: In modern JavaScript, you should generally **prefer** const **by default**. Use const whenever you know a variable's assignment won't need to change. If you *know* you'll need to reassign the variable later, use let. **Avoid using** var in new code unless you have a specific reason related to older environments or legacy codebases. Using let and const leads to clearer, more predictable code.

Naming Conventions

Choosing good names for your variables makes your code much easier to read and understand. Follow these conventions and rules:

- **Start with:** A letter (a-z, A-Z), an underscore (_), or a dollar sign ($). Cannot start with a number.
- **Can contain:** Letters, numbers, underscores, or dollar signs.
- **Case-sensitive:** myVariable is different from myvariable and MyVariable.
- **Reserved words:** You cannot use JavaScript's reserved keywords (like let, const, var, function, if, for, etc.) as variable names.
- **Convention (camelCase):** For multi-word variable names, the standard convention in JavaScript is **camelCase**. Start with a lowercase letter, and capitalize the first letter of each subsequent word (e.g., userName, totalAmount, isUserLoggedIn).
- **Be descriptive:** Choose names that clearly indicate the variable's purpose (e.g., firstName instead of fn, itemsInCart instead of iic).

```
// *Good variable names:*
let firstName = "Alice";
const itemsInCart = 3;
let isProcessingComplete = false;
let $element = /* ... */; // *Often used for DOM elements*
let _internalValue = /* ... */; // *Often used for "private" data*

// *Bad variable names (avoid these):*
// let 1stPlace = "Gold";    // *Cannot start with a number*
// let user name = "Bob";    // *Cannot contain spaces*
// let let = "oops";         // *Cannot use reserved words*
// let x = 100;              // *Not descriptive*
```

Primitive Data Types

Variables can hold different kinds of data. In JavaScript, the most basic kinds of data are called **primitive data types** (or primitives). Think of them as the fundamental atoms of information. JavaScript has several primitive types:

Strings

Strings represent textual data. You create strings by enclosing text within either single quotes ('...'), double quotes ("..."), or backticks (`...`).

```
let greeting = "Hello, world!";
let message = 'JavaScript is fun.';
let response = `Yes, it is!`; // *Backticks allow multi-line strings too*

console.log(greeting); // *Output: Hello, world!*
console.log(message);  // *Output: JavaScript is fun.*
```

You can combine strings using the + operator (concatenation):

```
let firstName = "Ada";
let lastName = "Lovelace";
let fullName = firstName + " " + lastName; // *Add a space in between*
console.log(fullName); // *Output: Ada Lovelace*
```

Backticks also enable **template literals**, a powerful feature allowing you to embed expressions (like variable values) directly within the string. We'll cover these in more detail in Chapter 18.

```
let city = "London";
let info = `I live in ${city}.`; // *Variable embedded using ${}*
console.log(info); // *Output: I live in London.*
```

Numbers

The number type represents numeric data, including integers and floating-point (decimal) numbers.

```
let age = 30;
let price = 19.99;
let temperature = -5;
```

```
let quantity = 10;
let totalCost = price * quantity; // *Basic calculation*

console.log(age);       // *Output: 30*
console.log(price);     // *Output: 19.99*
console.log(totalCost); // *Output: 199.9*
```

JavaScript numbers can also represent a few special values:

- `Infinity` and `-Infinity`: Represent mathematical infinity.
- `NaN`: Stands for "Not a Number". It typically results from invalid mathematical operations, like dividing by zero or trying to calculate with a non-numeric string.

```
console.log(1 / 0);      // *Output: Infinity*
console.log("hello" * 3);  // *Output: NaN*
```

We'll explore mathematical operations further in Chapter 3.

Booleans

Booleans represent logical values and can only be one of two things: `true` or `false`. They are essential for making decisions in your code, as we'll see in Chapter 4 (Conditional Statements).

```
let isLoggedIn = true;
let hasPermission = false;
let isComplete = 10 > 5; // *Comparison results in a boolean*

console.log(isLoggedIn); // *Output: true*
console.log(hasPermission); // *Output: false*
console.log(isComplete); // *Output: true*
```

Null and Undefined

These two types seem similar but represent different kinds of "emptiness" or "absence".

- `undefined`: Typically means a variable has been declared but has **not yet been assigned a value**. It's the default value for uninitialized variables, function parameters you don't provide, or object properties that don't exist.

```
let userEmail;
console.log(userEmail); // *Output: undefined*
```

- null: Represents the **intentional absence of any object value**. It's a value that you, the programmer, explicitly assign to indicate that a variable *should* have no value right now.

```
let selectedProduct = null; // *Explicitly set to 'no product selected'*
console.log(selectedProduct); // *Output: null*
```

Think of undefined as "haven't set a value yet" and null as "actively set to have no value".

Symbols and BigInts (A Brief Mention)

Modern JavaScript introduced two more primitive types:

- **Symbol:** Used to create unique identifiers, often for object properties, preventing naming collisions.
- **BigInt:** Used to represent integers larger than the maximum safe integer value that the standard number type can reliably handle.

These are more advanced types, and you likely won't need them when you're just starting. We'll focus on Strings, Numbers, Booleans, Null, and Undefined for now.

Checking Types with typeof

Sometimes, you need to know what type of data a variable holds. JavaScript provides the typeof operator for this purpose. It returns a string indicating the type of the operand (the value or variable you give it).

```
let name = "Gandalf";
let level = 99;
let isWizard = true;
let inventory = null;
let quest; // *undefined*

console.log(typeof name);     // *Output: "string"*
console.log(typeof level);    // *Output: "number"*
console.log(typeof isWizard); // *Output: "boolean"*
console.log(typeof quest);    // *Output: "undefined"*
```

```
// *A known quirk of JavaScript:*
console.log(typeof inventory); // *Output: "object" (not "null")*

console.log(typeof NaN);        // *Output: "number"*
console.log(typeof Symbol('id')); // *Output: "symbol"*
console.log(typeof 100n);       // *Output: "bigint"*
```

Notice the odd result for `typeof null`. For historical reasons, `typeof null` returns `"object"`. This is a long-standing bug that can't easily be fixed without breaking existing web code, so you just need to remember this exception.

A Note on Type Coercion

JavaScript is known as a **dynamically typed** language. This means you don't have to explicitly declare the *type* of a variable when you create it (like you might in some other languages). JavaScript figures out the type automatically based on the value you assign.

Furthermore, JavaScript sometimes tries to be "helpful" by automatically converting values from one type to another in certain situations. This is called **type coercion** or type conversion.

For example:

```
let result = "The answer is: " + 42;
console.log(result); // *Output: "The answer is: 42"*
// *JavaScript coerced the number 42 into the string "42" to perform
concatenation.*

let calculation = "5" * 3;
console.log(calculation); // *Output: 15*
// *Here, JavaScript coerced the string "5" into the number 5 for
multiplication.*

let tricky = "5" + 3;
console.log(tricky); // *Output: "53"*
// *But with +, if one operand is a string, it prefers concatenation!*
```

While sometimes convenient, implicit type coercion can also lead to unexpected results and subtle bugs if you're not careful. We will explore type coercion and how to perform explicit type conversions in more detail later in the book. For now, just be aware that it happens.

Chapter Summary

In this chapter, we unpacked the essential building blocks of JavaScript. We learned that programs are sequences of **statements**, often ending in semicolons. We saw how to use **comments** (`//` and `/* */`) to add explanations to our code. The core concept of **variables** (`let`, `const`, `var`) as named containers for data was introduced, along with best practices for naming them (camelCase) and the recommendation to favor `const` and `let` over `var`. We then explored the fundamental **primitive data types**: `string`, `number`, `boolean`, `null`, and `undefined`. Finally, we learned how to check a value's type using the `typeof` operator and got a first glimpse at JavaScript's automatic type coercion.

You now understand how to declare pieces of information and give them labels. But simply storing data isn't enough; we need to *do* things with it! In the next chapter, we'll dive into **operators** – the symbols that allow us to perform calculations, compare values, assign data, and combine logical conditions, truly bringing our variables and values to life.

3

Operators

In the last chapter, we learned how to store different kinds of information using variables and primitive data types like strings, numbers, and booleans. That's like gathering ingredients for a recipe. But ingredients alone don't make a meal; you need actions – mixing, heating, chopping. Similarly, in JavaScript, just having data isn't enough. We need ways to work with that data, perform calculations, make comparisons, and combine conditions. This is where **operators** come in. Think of operators as the action symbols in JavaScript; they take our variables and values (called operands) and perform specific operations on them, producing a result. This chapter introduces the essential operators you'll use constantly to bring your code to life.

Arithmetic Operators

Let's start with the most familiar group: arithmetic operators. These perform standard mathematical calculations on number values.

Operator	Name	Description	Example	Result
+	Addition	Adds two numbers	5 + 3	8
-	Subtraction	Subtracts the second number from the first	10 - 4	6
*	Multiplication	Multiplies two numbers	6 * 7	42
/	Division	Divides the first number by the second	20 / 5	4

%	Remainder (Modulo)	Returns the remainder of a division	`10 % 3`	`1`
**	Exponentiation	Raises the first number to the power of the second	`2 ** 4`	`16`
++	Increment	Increases a number variable by 1	`let a = 5;` `a++;`	a becomes 6
--	Decrement	Decreases a number variable by 1	`let b = 9;` `b--;`	b becomes 8

```
let apples = 12;
let oranges = 8;

let totalFruit = apples + oranges; // *Addition*
console.log(totalFruit); // *Output: 20*

let difference = apples - oranges; // *Subtraction*
console.log(difference); // *Output: 4*

let costPerApple = 0.5;
let totalCost = apples * costPerApple; // *Multiplication*
console.log(totalCost); // *Output: 6*

let applesPerPerson = apples / 4; // *Division*
console.log(applesPerPerson); // *Output: 3*

let items = 10;
let groupSize = 3;
let remainingItems = items % groupSize;
console.log(remainingItems); // *Output: 1 (10 divided by 3 is 3, remainder 1)*

let powerOfTwo = 2 ** 5; // *Exponentiation (2*2*2*2*2)*
console.log(powerOfTwo); // *Output: 32*

// *Increment and Decrement*
let score = 100;
score++; // *Increment: score becomes 101*
console.log(score); // *Output: 101*

let lives = 3;
lives--; // *Decrement: lives becomes 2*
console.log(lives); // *Output: 2*
```

A Note on Increment/Decrement: ++ and -- can be placed *before* (prefix: ++score) or *after* (postfix: score++) the variable. While both increment/decrement the variable, they differ in the value they *return* in the expression where they are used. Postfix returns the original value *before* changing it, while prefix returns the *new* value. For simplicity now, using them on their own line (like `score++;`) avoids this complexity.

Operator Precedence: Just like in regular math, JavaScript operators have an order of precedence. Multiplication (*), division (/), and remainder (%) are performed before addition (+) and subtraction (-). Exponentiation (**) often happens even earlier.

```
let result = 3 + 4 * 5; // *Multiplication happens first (4 * 5 = 20)*
console.log(result);    // *Output: 23 (not 35)*
```

If you want to override the default precedence, use parentheses (). Operations inside parentheses are always evaluated first.

```
let resultWithParens = (3 + 4) * 5; // *Addition happens first (3 + 4 = 7)*
console.log(resultWithParens);      // *Output: 35*
```

Assignment Operators

We've already used the most basic assignment operator: the single equals sign (=). It assigns the value on its right to the variable on its left.

```
let currentLevel = 1; // *Assigns 1 to currentLevel*
let playerName = "Link"; // *Assigns "Link" to playerName*
```

JavaScript also provides **compound assignment operators** that combine an arithmetic operation with assignment for more concise code.

Operator	Example	Equivalent To
+=	x += y	x = x + y
-=	x -= y	x = x - y
*=	x *= y	x = x * y
/=	x /= y	x = x / y
%=	x %= y	x = x % y
**=	x **= y	x = x ** y

```
let currentScore = 50;
let pointsEarned = 25;
```

```
currentScore += pointsEarned; // *Equivalent to: currentScore = currentScore +
pointsEarned;*
console.log(currentScore); // *Output: 75*

let fuel = 100;
let fuelUsed = 15;

fuel -= fuelUsed; // *Equivalent to: fuel = fuel - fuelUsed;*
console.log(fuel); // *Output: 85*

let quantity = 5;
quantity *= 2; // *Equivalent to: quantity = quantity * 2;*
console.log(quantity); // *Output: 10*
```

These shorthand operators make common operations like updating counters or totals cleaner and easier to read.

Comparison Operators

Often, we need to compare values to make decisions in our code. Comparison operators evaluate two operands and return a boolean value: true or false.

Operator	Name	Description	Example (x=5)	Result
==	Equal (Loose)	Checks if values are equal (performs type coercion)	x == 8	0
			x == 5	1
			x == "5"	1
===	Strict Equal	Checks if values AND types are equal (no coercion)	x === 5	1
			x === "5"	0
!=	Not Equal (Loose)	Checks if values are not equal (coercion)	x != 8	1
			x != "5"	0
!==	Strict Not Equal	Checks if values OR types are not equal	x !== 5	0
			x !== "5"	1
			x !== 8	1
>	Greater Than		x > 8	0
<	Less Than		x < 8	1

>=	Greater Than or Equal To		x >= 8	0
			x >= 5	1
<=	Less Than or Equal To		x <= 8	1

```
let userAge = 25;
let votingAge = 18;

console.log(userAge > votingAge); // *Output: true*
console.log(userAge === votingAge); // *Output: false*
console.log(userAge !== votingAge); // *Output: true*

let itemPrice = 50;
let budget = 50;
console.log(itemPrice <= budget); // *Output: true*
```

Loose Equality (==) vs. Strict Equality (===)

This is a crucial distinction in JavaScript!

- **Loose Equality (==):** Tries to compare values *after* attempting to convert them to a common type (type coercion). This can lead to unexpected results.
- **Strict Equality (===):** Compares both the value *and* the data type. It does **not** perform type coercion. If the types are different, it immediately returns false.

```
console.log(5 == "5");    // *Output: true (String "5" is coerced to number 5)*
console.log(5 === "5");   // *Output: false (Number type is different from String type)*

console.log(0 == false); // *Output: true (false is coerced to 0)*
console.log(0 === false);// *Output: false (Number type is different from Boolean type)*

console.log(null == undefined); // *Output: true (A special case for loose equality)*
console.log(null === undefined);// *Output: false (Different types)*
```

Best Practice: Almost always use strict equality (===) and strict inequality (!==). This makes your code more predictable and avoids bugs caused by unintentional type coercion. Only use loose equality (==) if you have a very specific reason to allow type coercion in a comparison.

Logical Operators

Logical operators work primarily with boolean values (`true` or `false`) and are used to combine multiple conditions or invert a single condition. They are fundamental for building the decision-making logic we'll see in Chapter 4.

1. **Logical AND (&&)**: Returns `true` only if **both** operands are `true`. Otherwise, it returns `false`.

    ```
    let loggedIn = true;
    let hasAdminRights = false;
    let canAccessResource = loggedIn && hasAdminRights;

    console.log(canAccessResource); // *Output: false (true && false)*

    let isWeekend = true;
    let weatherIsGood = true;
    let goToPark = isWeekend && weatherIsGood;

    console.log(goToPark); // *Output: true (true && true)*
    ```

2. **Logical OR (||)**: Returns `true` if **at least one** of the operands is `true`. It only returns `false` if *both* operands are `false`.

    ```
    let hasCoupon = false;
    let isMember = true;
    let canGetDiscount = hasCoupon || isMember;

    console.log(canGetDiscount); // *Output: true (false || true)*

    let missedAlarm = false;
    let isHoliday = false;
    let sleepIn = missedAlarm || isHoliday;

    console.log(sleepIn); // *Output: false (false || false)*
    ```

3. **Logical NOT (!)**: Inverts the boolean value of its operand. It turns `true` into `false` and `false` into `true`.

    ```
    let isRaining = true;
    let notRaining = !isRaining;

    console.log(notRaining); // *Output: false*
    ```

```
let filesSaved = false;
let canCloseWindow = !filesSaved; // *Maybe you check this before
closing*

console.log(canCloseWindow); // *Output: true*
```

Short-Circuiting: Logical AND (&&) and OR (||) operators exhibit "short-circuiting" behavior.

- For &&, if the first operand is false, the result *must* be false, so JavaScript doesn't even evaluate the second operand.
- For ||, if the first operand is true, the result *must* be true, so JavaScript doesn't evaluate the second operand. This can be useful for performance and for preventing errors (e.g., trying to access a property on a null object).

The Ternary Operator

The conditional (or ternary) operator is the only JavaScript operator that takes three operands. It provides a concise way to write simple conditional assignments, acting as a shorthand for a basic if...else statement (which we'll cover fully in Chapter 4).

The syntax is: `condition ? valueIfTrue : valueIfFalse`

1. A condition is evaluated.
2. If the condition is true, the operator resolves to valueIfTrue.
3. If the condition is false, the operator resolves to valueIfFalse.

```
let age = 20;
let beverage = (age >= 21) ? "Beer" : "Juice";
// *Condition (age >= 21) is false, so it takes the value after :*
console.log(beverage); // *Output: "Juice"*

let isAuthenticated = true;
let greeting = isAuthenticated ? "Welcome back!" : "Please log in.";
// *Condition (isAuthenticated) is true, so it takes the value after ?*
console.log(greeting); // *Output: "Welcome back!"*
```

While concise, overuse of nested or complex ternary operators can make code harder to read than a standard if...else block. Use it for straightforward conditional assignments.

Other Useful Operators

JavaScript has several other operators, some of which we've encountered or will explore later:

- `typeof`: We saw this in Chapter 2. It returns a string indicating the data type of an operand.

  ```
  console.log(typeof 100); // *Output: "number"*
  ```

- `instanceof`: Checks if an object is an instance of a particular constructor or class (more relevant when we discuss objects and classes).
- `delete`: Removes a property from an object.
- **Comma Operator (,)**: Allows multiple expressions to be evaluated in a sequence, returning the result of the last expression. Less commonly used directly but appears in some `for` loop constructs (Chapter 5).
- **Bitwise Operators (&, |, ^, ~, <<, >>, >>>)**: Perform operations directly on the binary representation of numbers. These are less common in everyday web development but used in specific low-level or performance-critical scenarios.

Don't worry about memorizing all of these less common operators right now. Focus on mastering the arithmetic, assignment, comparison, and logical operators, as they form the backbone of most JavaScript logic.

Chapter Summary

This chapter armed you with the "action words" of JavaScript: operators. We started with **arithmetic operators** (+, -, *, /, %, **, ++, --) for performing calculations, keeping operator precedence and parentheses in mind. Then, we covered **assignment operators** (=, +=, -=, etc.) for storing values and updating variables concisely. A crucial part was understanding **comparison operators** (>, <, ===, !==, etc.), especially the vital difference between strict (===) and loose (==) equality, emphasizing the preference for strict comparison. We explored **logical operators** (&&, ||, !) for combining or inverting boolean conditions, noting their short-circuiting behavior. Finally, we introduced the **ternary operator** (? :) as a shorthand for simple conditional assignments and acknowledged other operators like `typeof`.

You can now not only store data but also manipulate it, compare it, and combine logical outcomes. These operators, particularly the comparison and logical ones, are the essential tools needed for the next step: controlling the flow of your program based on conditions. In Chapter 4, we will delve into **conditional statements** (`if`, `else if`, `else`, `switch`), where you'll heavily utilize these operators to make your JavaScript code make decisions and react dynamically.

4

Making Decisions

Life is full of choices, and so is programming! Rarely does a program execute the exact same sequence of instructions every time. Think about your daily routine: if it's raining, you grab an umbrella; if it's a weekday, you set an alarm; otherwise, you might sleep in. Computer programs constantly need to make similar decisions based on the data they have or the input they receive. In the previous chapter, we learned about operators, especially comparison (===, >, etc.) and logical (&&, ||, !) operators, which allow us to ask questions about our data and get `true` or `false` answers. Now, we'll learn how to use those answers to control which parts of our code actually run. This chapter introduces **conditional statements**, the structures that allow your JavaScript programs to make decisions and follow different paths based on specific conditions.

The if Statement

The most fundamental conditional statement is the `if` statement. It allows you to execute a block of code *only if* a specific condition evaluates to `true`.

The basic structure looks like this:

```
if (condition) {
  // *Code to execute if the condition is true*
}
// *Code here runs regardless of the condition*
```

1. The keyword if signals the start of the statement.
2. The condition is placed inside parentheses (). This condition is typically an expression that evaluates to a boolean (true or false), often using the comparison and logical operators we learned in Chapter 3.
3. If the condition is true, the code inside the following curly braces {} (the code block) is executed.
4. If the condition is false, the code inside the curly braces is skipped entirely, and the program continues with any code *after* the if block.

Let's see an example:

```
let temperature = 30; // *Degrees Celsius*

if (temperature > 25) {
  console.log("It's a hot day! Wear shorts.");
}

console.log("Checking the weather is done.");

// *Output:*
// It's a hot day! Wear shorts.
// Checking the weather is done.
```

In this case, temperature > 25 (30 > 25) is true, so the message inside the curly braces is printed. Now, let's see what happens if the condition is false:

```
let temperature = 15; // *Degrees Celsius*

if (temperature > 25) {
  // *This condition (15 > 25) is false*
  console.log("It's a hot day! Wear shorts.");
}

console.log("Checking the weather is done.");

// *Output:*
// Checking the weather is done.
```

Here, temperature > 25 is false, so the console.log inside the if block is skipped.

Adding Alternatives

The if statement is great for doing something *only* when a condition is true. But what if you want to do something *else* when the condition is false? That's where the else keyword comes in. You add an else block immediately after the if block's closing curly brace.

```
if (condition) {
  // *Code to execute if the condition is true*
} else {
  // *Code to execute if the condition is false*
}
```

The else block provides an alternative path – its code runs *only* when the if condition evaluates to false.

```
let userAge = 17;
const votingAge = 18;

if (userAge >= votingAge) {
  console.log("You are eligible to vote.");
} else {
  console.log("You are not yet eligible to vote.");
}

// *Output:*
// You are not yet eligible to vote.
```

Since userAge >= votingAge (17 >= 18) is false, the code inside the else block is executed. One, and *only* one, of the blocks (if or else) will run.

Multiple Choices

Sometimes, you have more than just two possibilities. You might need to check several conditions in sequence. For this, you can chain if and else statements using else if.

```
if (condition1) {
  // *Code if condition1 is true*
} else if (condition2) {
  // *Code if condition1 is false AND condition2 is true*
} else if (condition3) {
```

```
  // *Code if conditions 1 and 2 are false AND condition3 is true*
} else {
  // *Code if ALL previous conditions are false*
}
```

JavaScript evaluates the conditions one by one from top to bottom:

1. It checks `condition1`. If `true`, its block runs, and the rest of the chain (`else if`, `else`) is skipped.
2. If `condition1` is `false`, it checks `condition2`. If `true`, its block runs, and the rest is skipped.
3. This continues down the `else if` chain.
4. If *none* of the `if` or `else if` conditions are `true`, the final `else` block (if present) runs. The final `else` is optional.

Let's model a simple grading system:

```
let score = 78;
let grade;

if (score >= 90) {
  grade = "A";
} else if (score >= 80) { // *Checked only if score < 90*
  grade = "B";
} else if (score >= 70) { // *Checked only if score < 80*
  grade = "C";
} else if (score >= 60) { // *Checked only if score < 70*
  grade = "D";
} else {                  // *Runs only if score < 60*
  grade = "F";
}

console.log(`Your grade is: ${grade}`);

// *Output:*
// Your grade is: C
```

Because `score` is 78:

- `score >= 90` (78 >= 90) is `false`.
- `score >= 80` (78 >= 80) is `false`.
- `score >= 70` (78 >= 70) is `true`. The code `grade = "C"` runs, and the rest of the `else if` and `else` blocks are skipped.

Truthy and Falsy Values Revisited

Now, a slightly tricky but very important aspect of conditions in JavaScript. The `if` condition doesn't strictly require a boolean (`true` or `false`). It will actually evaluate *any* expression. If the expression's result isn't already a boolean, JavaScript implicitly tries to convert it into one using a concept called **truthiness**.

Most values in JavaScript, when used in a boolean context like an `if` statement, are considered "truthy" – they coerce to `true`. However, a few specific values are considered **falsy** – they coerce to `false`.

The primary **falsy** values you need to remember are:

- `false` (the boolean value itself)
- `0` (the number zero)
- `-0` (negative zero)
- `0n` (BigInt zero)
- `""` (an empty string)
- `null`
- `undefined`
- `NaN` (Not a Number)

All other values are truthy, including:

- Any non-empty string (`"hello"`, `"0"`, `"false"`)
- Any non-zero number (`1`, `-10`, `0.5`)
- Arrays (`[]`, even if empty)
- Objects (`{}`, even if empty)
- The boolean `true`

Let's see this in action:

```
let userName = ""; // *Empty string - falsy*
if (userName) {
  console.log(`Welcome, ${userName}!`); // *This won't run*
} else {
  console.log("Please enter your username."); // *This will run*
}
// *Output: Please enter your username.*

let itemsInCart = 5; // *Non-zero number - truthy*
if (itemsInCart) {
  console.log(`You have ${itemsInCart} items in your cart.`); // *This runs*
```

```
} else {
  console.log("Your cart is empty.");
}
// *Output: You have 5 items in your cart.*

let selectedItem = null; // *null - falsy*
if (selectedItem) {
  console.log("Processing item..."); // *This won't run*
} else {
  console.log("No item selected."); // *This will run*
}
// *Output: No item selected.*
```

Understanding truthy and falsy values allows you to write concise checks, like checking if a user has entered *any* text for their name (if (userName)), or if a quantity is greater than zero (if (quantity)). However, be mindful that relying on truthiness can sometimes be less explicit than a direct comparison (e.g., if (itemsInCart > 0) might be clearer than if (itemsInCart) depending on context).

A Different Kind of Choice

When you have a single value or expression that you need to compare against multiple *specific*, distinct possibilities, using a long chain of if...else if...else statements can become repetitive and sometimes hard to read. The switch statement offers an alternative structure for such cases.

The basic syntax is:

```
switch (expression) {
  case value1:
    // *Code to run if expression === value1*
    break; // *Important: stops execution within the switch*
  case value2:
    // *Code to run if expression === value2*
    break;
  case value3:
    // *Code to run if expression === value3*
    break;
  // ... more cases
  default:
    // *Code to run if expression matches none of the cases*
    // *The default case is optional*
}
```

1. The `switch` keyword starts the statement, followed by the `expression` to be evaluated (placed in parentheses).
2. The value of the `expression` is then compared strictly (`===`) against the value following each `case` keyword.
3. If a match is found (e.g., `expression === value1`), the code block following that `case` (down to the `break` statement) is executed.
4. The `break` statement is crucial. It tells JavaScript to exit the `switch` statement immediately after the matched case's code has run. **If you omit** `break`, execution will "fall through" to the *next* case block, regardless of whether its value matches, which is usually not what you want!
5. The `default` case is optional. Its code block runs if the `expression` does not match *any* of the preceding `case` values. It's similar to the final `else` in an `if...else if` chain.

Let's look at an example handling user menu choices:

```
let userChoice = "edit";
let actionMessage;

switch (userChoice) {
  case "view":
    actionMessage = "Displaying content...";
    break;
  case "edit":
    actionMessage = "Opening editor...";
    break; // *Without this, it would fall through to "delete"!*
  case "delete":
    actionMessage = "Are you sure you want to delete?";
    break;
  case "share":
    actionMessage = "Opening sharing options...";
    break;
  default:
    actionMessage = "Invalid choice selected.";
}

console.log(actionMessage);

// *Output:*
// Opening editor...
```

If `userChoice` was "delete", the output would be "Are you sure you want to delete?". If `userChoice` was "save", it wouldn't match any case, so the `default` block would run, outputting "Invalid choice selected.".

When to use switch **vs** if/else if?

- Use switch when checking a single variable or expression against several **discrete, known values** (like specific strings or numbers).
- Use if / else if when dealing with **ranges** (e.g., score >= 90), complex boolean conditions, or when comparing different variables in different conditions.

Combining Conditions

Remember the logical operators (&&, ||, !) from Chapter 3? You can use them inside the conditions of your if, else if statements to create more complex decision logic.

```
let hour = 14; // *2 PM*
let isWeekend = false;

// *Check if it's lunchtime on a weekday*
if (hour >= 12 && hour < 13 && !isWeekend) {
  console.log("Time for your lunch break!");
} else {
  console.log("Keep working (or relaxing if it's the weekend!)");
}
// *Output: Keep working (or relaxing if it's the weekend!)*

let hasValidLicense = true;
let hasCar = false;
let hasBike = true;

// *Check if the person can commute using their own vehicle*
if (hasValidLicense && (hasCar || hasBike)) {
  // *Note the parentheses for clarity with OR*
  console.log("You can commute with your own vehicle.");
} else {
  console.log("You might need public transport or a ride.");
}
// *Output: You can commute with your own vehicle.*
```

By combining conditions, you can model intricate real-world rules and scenarios within your code.

Chapter Summary

In this chapter, we explored how to give our JavaScript programs the ability to make decisions. We learned the fundamental `if` statement for executing code based on a true condition, the `else` statement for providing an alternative path when the condition is false, and the `else if` structure for checking multiple conditions sequentially. We revisited the important concepts of **truthy and falsy** values, understanding how JavaScript evaluates non-boolean conditions. We also introduced the `switch` statement as a useful alternative to `if...else if` chains when comparing a single expression against multiple specific values, highlighting the critical role of the `break` statement. Finally, we saw how **logical operators** (`&&`, `||`, `!`) can be used within conditions to build more complex decision-making logic.

You can now control the flow of execution, making your programs respond dynamically to different situations. However, sometimes you need to perform an action repeatedly. Instead of writing the same code multiple times, we need a way to loop. In the next chapter, we'll dive into **loops** (`for`, `while`, `do...while`), which allow you to execute blocks of code multiple times efficiently.

5

Repeating Actions

In the previous chapter, we learned how to make our programs make decisions using conditional statements (`if`, `else`, `switch`). This allows for different paths of execution. But what if you need to perform the same task, or a very similar task, multiple times? Imagine sending a personalized greeting to 100 users, or calculating the sum of numbers from 1 to 50, or checking every item in a shopping list. Writing the code for each repetition individually would be incredibly tedious, error-prone, and inefficient. This is where **loops** come to the rescue! Loops are fundamental control structures in JavaScript that allow you to execute a block of code repeatedly until a certain condition is met. They are the key to automating repetitive tasks.

Why Use Loops?

Loops embody a core programming principle known as **DRY - Don't Repeat Yourself**. Instead of copying and pasting similar code blocks, you write the code *once* inside a loop structure and tell JavaScript how many times, or under what conditions, it should be repeated.

Using loops offers several advantages:

- **Conciseness:** Reduces the amount of code you need to write.
- **Readability:** Often makes the intent of the code clearer (e.g., "process all items" is clearer than 100 lines of processing code).

- **Maintainability**: If you need to change the repeated task, you only need to modify it in one place (inside the loop body).
- **Flexibility**: Loops can handle situations where the number of repetitions isn't known beforehand.

JavaScript provides several types of loops, each suited for different scenarios. Let's explore the most common ones.

The `for` Loop

The `for` loop is often the go-to choice when you know **how many times** you want the loop to run. It's like saying, "Do this task exactly 10 times."

The basic syntax looks a bit more complex than `if`, but it's very structured:

```
for (initialization; condition; final-expression) {
  // Code block to be executed repeatedly (loop body)
}
```

Let's break down the three parts inside the parentheses, separated by semicolons:

1. `initialization`: This expression is executed **once** before the loop starts. It's typically used to declare and initialize a counter variable (often named `i` for "index" or "iterator").
2. `condition`: This expression is evaluated **before each potential loop iteration**.
    - If the condition is `true`, the code inside the loop body (`{...}`) executes.
    - If the condition becomes `false`, the loop terminates, and the program continues with the code *after* the loop.
3. `final-expression`: This expression is executed **at the end of each loop iteration**, *after* the loop body runs. It's typically used to update the counter variable (e.g., increment it).

Here's a classic example: counting from 1 to 5:

```
console.log("Starting the loop!");

for (let i = 1; i <= 5; i++) {
  // initialization: let i = 1; (runs once)
  // condition: i <= 5 (checked before each iteration)
  // final-expression: i++ (runs after each iteration body)
```

```
    console.log(`Current count is: ${i}`);
}

console.log("Loop finished!");

// *Output:*
// Starting the loop!
// Current count is: 1
// Current count is: 2
// Current count is: 3
// Current count is: 4
// Current count is: 5
// Loop finished!
```

How it works:

1. `let i = 1;` initializes i to 1.
2. `i <= 5` (1 <= 5) is `true`. Loop body runs: prints "Current count is: 1".
3. `i++` executes. i becomes 2.
4. `i <= 5` (2 <= 5) is `true`. Loop body runs: prints "Current count is: 2".
5. `i++` executes. i becomes 3.
6. `i <= 5` (3 <= 5) is `true`. Loop body runs: prints "Current count is: 3".
7. `i++` executes. i becomes 4.
8. `i <= 5` (4 <= 5) is `true`. Loop body runs: prints "Current count is: 4".
9. `i++` executes. i becomes 5.
10. `i <= 5` (5 <= 5) is `true`. Loop body runs: prints "Current count is: 5".
11. `i++` executes. i becomes 6.
12. `i <= 5` (6 <= 5) is `false`. The loop terminates.
13. "Loop finished!" is printed.

The variable declared in the `initialization` part (`let i`) is typically scoped to the loop itself, meaning it doesn't exist outside the loop (this is a benefit of using `let` or `const` here, which we discussed in Chapter 2 and will revisit in Chapter 9 on Scope).

The `while` Loop

What if you don't know exactly how many times you need to loop? Maybe you need to keep doing something *until* a specific condition is met, like waiting for user input or processing items until a resource is depleted. For these scenarios, the `while` loop is ideal.

The `while` loop is simpler in structure than the `for` loop:

```
while (condition) {
  // Code block to execute as long as the condition is true

  // *Crucial: Something inside the loop must eventually*
  // *make the condition false, otherwise it's an infinite loop!*
}
```

1. The keyword while starts the loop.
2. The condition inside the parentheses is evaluated **before** each potential iteration.
3. If the condition is true, the code block executes.
4. After the block executes, the condition is checked *again*. This cycle repeats.
5. If (or when) the condition evaluates to false, the loop stops, and the program continues after the loop block.

Let's simulate a simple countdown:

```
let countdown = 3;

console.log("Starting countdown...");

while (countdown > 0) {
  console.log(countdown);
  countdown--; // *Decrement the counter - vital step!*
}

console.log("Blast off!");

// *Output:*
// Starting countdown...
// 3
// 2
// 1
// Blast off!
```

How it works:

1. countdown > 0 (3 > 0) is true. Prints 3. countdown becomes 2.
2. countdown > 0 (2 > 0) is true. Prints 2. countdown becomes 1.
3. countdown > 0 (1 > 0) is true. Prints 1. countdown becomes 0.
4. countdown > 0 (0 > 0) is false. The loop terminates.
5. "Blast off!" is printed.

Crucially, notice the `countdown--` line. Without it, `countdown` would always remain 3, `countdown > 0` would always be true, and the loop would run forever! This is called an **infinite loop**, which we'll discuss more shortly.

The `do...while` Loop

The `do...while` loop is a close relative of the `while` loop. The key difference is that the condition is checked **after** the loop body executes, not before. This guarantees that the code inside the loop block will run **at least once**, even if the condition is initially false.

The syntax is:

```
do {
  // Code block to execute

  // *Again, ensure something can make the condition false*
} while (condition); // *Semicolon is required here!*
```

1. The keyword do starts the loop.
2. The code block {...} executes **first**.
3. Then, the `condition` inside the `while()` parentheses is evaluated.
4. If the `condition` is `true`, execution jumps back to the do block for another iteration.
5. If the `condition` is `false`, the loop terminates.

When would you use this? A common scenario is prompting a user for input until they provide something valid, ensuring the prompt appears at least once.

```
let userInput;

do {
  // *Assume prompt() is a function that gets user input (we'll see DOM
interaction later)*
  // *For now, let's simulate it*
  console.log("Please enter 'yes' or 'no':");
  // *In a real scenario, you'd get input here. Let's simulate a few tries.*
  if (userInput === undefined) {
      userInput = "maybe"; // *First invalid try*
      console.log(`Simulated input: ${userInput}`);
  } else if (userInput === "maybe") {
      userInput = "yes"; // *Second valid try*
       console.log(`Simulated input: ${userInput}`);
```

```
    }

} while (userInput !== "yes" && userInput !== "no");

console.log(`You entered: ${userInput}`);

// *Output:*
// Please enter 'yes' or 'no':
// Simulated input: maybe
// Please enter 'yes' or 'no':
// Simulated input: yes
// You entered: yes
```

Notice the loop ran twice: once with the invalid "maybe", and again to get the valid "yes". If userInput had been initialized to "yes" *before* the loop, the do block would still have run once before the condition was checked.

Avoiding Infinite Loops

An infinite loop occurs when the loop's exit condition is never met. The loop runs forever (or until the browser/system intervenes, often by freezing or crashing). This is usually a bug!

Common Causes:

- while / do...while: Forgetting to include code inside the loop that changes the variable(s) involved in the condition, so the condition *never* becomes false.

    ```
    // *Infinite loop - danger!*
    let count = 0;
    while (count < 10) {
      console.log("Still going...");
      // *Forgot to increment count (e.g., count++;)*
    }
    ```

- for: Writing a condition or final-expression that doesn't progress towards making the condition false.

    ```
    // *Infinite loop - danger!*
    for (let i = 0; i < 5; i--) { // *Decrementing i makes it always less
    than 5*
      console.log("Going the wrong way!");
    }
    ```

Prevention:

- Always double-check that the variables in your loop condition are being modified within the loop body (`while`, `do...while`) or in the final-expression (`for`) in a way that will eventually make the condition false.
- Test your loops carefully, perhaps with a temporary counter or `console.log` statements, to ensure they terminate as expected.

If you accidentally run an infinite loop in a browser tab, you might need to close that tab or even force-quit the browser.

Controlling Loops

Sometimes, you need more granular control over your loops than just letting them run until the main condition is met. JavaScript provides two statements for this: `break` and `continue`.

break

We encountered `break` in the `switch` statement (Chapter 4). In the context of loops (`for`, `while`, `do...while`), the `break` statement **immediately terminates the entire loop**, regardless of whether the loop's main condition is still true. Execution continues with the first statement *after* the loop block.

It's often used when you're searching for something and want to stop as soon as you find it.

```
let numbers = [2, 5, 8, 12, 15, 20]; // *An array (more in Chapter 6)*
let foundNumber = -1; // *Default value if not found*
let searchTarget = 12;

console.log(`Searching for ${searchTarget}...`);

for (let i = 0; i < numbers.length; i++) { // *Loop through array indices*
  console.log(`Checking index ${i}, value ${numbers[i]}`);
  if (numbers[i] === searchTarget) {
    foundNumber = numbers[i];
    console.log("Found it!");
    break; // *Exit the loop immediately*
  }
}

if (foundNumber !== -1) {
```

```
        console.log(`Target ${foundNumber} was located.`);
} else {
        console.log(`Target ${searchTarget} not in the list.`);
}

// *Output:*
// Searching for 12...
// Checking index 0, value 2
// Checking index 1, value 5
// Checking index 2, value 8
// Checking index 3, value 12
// Found it!
// Target 12 was located.
```

Notice how the loop stopped checking 15 and 20 once 12 was found and break was executed.

continue

The continue statement doesn't terminate the entire loop. Instead, it **skips the rest of the code inside the current iteration** of the loop body and immediately proceeds to the **next iteration** (evaluating the condition and running the final-expression in a for loop).

It's useful when you want to process most items in a loop but skip certain ones based on a condition.

Example: Print only the odd numbers between 1 and 10.

```
console.log("Printing odd numbers:");

for (let i = 1; i <= 10; i++) {
  if (i % 2 === 0) { // *Check if the number is even*
    continue; // *Skip the rest of this iteration if even*
  }
  // *This line is only reached if the 'continue' was NOT executed (i.e., if i
is odd)*
  console.log(i);
}

// *Output:*
// Printing odd numbers:
// 1
// 3
// 5
```

```
// 7
// 9
```

When i was 2, 4, 6, 8, or 10, the if condition was true, continue was executed, and the console.log(i) line was skipped for that iteration.

Looping Through Collections (An Early Look)

One of the most common uses for loops is to process collections of data, like lists of items. In JavaScript, the primary way to represent ordered lists is using **Arrays**. While we'll dedicate Chapter 6 entirely to arrays, let's quickly see how a for loop is perfectly suited for iterating over them.

Arrays have a length property that tells you how many items they contain, and you access individual items using numerical indexes starting from 0.

```
let colors = ["red", "green", "blue", "yellow"];

console.log("Available colors:");

// *Loop from index 0 up to (but not including) colors.length*
for (let i = 0; i < colors.length; i++) {
  let currentColor = colors[i]; // *Access element at index i*
  console.log(`- ${currentColor}`);
}

// *Output:*
// Available colors:
// - red
// - green
// - blue
// - yellow
```

This pattern (using a for loop with an index from 0 to array.length - 1) is fundamental for working with arrays. We'll explore this and more convenient ways to loop over arrays in later chapters.

Chapter Summary

This chapter introduced the powerful concept of **loops** for automating repetitive tasks. We covered the for **loop**, ideal when you know the number of repetitions, breaking down its `initialization`, `condition`, and `final-expression` components. We explored the `while` **loop** for repeating tasks as long as a condition remains true, emphasizing the need to ensure the condition eventually becomes false. The `do...while` **loop** was presented as a variant that guarantees at least one execution before checking the condition. We discussed the critical importance of **avoiding infinite loops** and how they commonly occur. Finally, we learned how to gain finer control within loops using `break` to exit early and `continue` to skip the current iteration. We also got a glimpse of how loops, particularly `for` loops, are essential for working with collections like arrays.

You now have the tools to not only make decisions (`if/else`) but also to repeat actions efficiently (`for/while`). These control flow structures are the core logic builders in programming. With variables, operators, conditions, and loops under your belt, you're ready to start organizing data more effectively. In the next chapter, we'll dive deep into **Arrays**, JavaScript's primary tool for storing ordered lists of data, and see how loops make working with them practical.

So far, we've learned how to store single pieces of information using variables (Chapter 2) and how to repeat actions using loops (Chapter 5). Variables are great for holding individual items like a user's name or the current temperature. But what happens when you need to work with a *collection* of related items? Imagine needing to store a list of student names, the high scores for a game, the steps in a recipe, or the colors available for a product. Creating a separate variable for each item (`score1`, `score2`, `score3`, ...) would quickly become unmanageable, especially if the list size can change.

This is where **Arrays** come into play. Arrays are a fundamental data structure in JavaScript used to store an **ordered list** of multiple values under a single variable name. Think of an array like a numbered list or a shelf with specifically numbered slots, where each slot can hold a value.

What is an Array?

An array is a special type of object in JavaScript specifically designed to hold a collection of items in a particular sequence. Key characteristics include:

- **Ordered:** The items in an array maintain a specific order. The first item you add stays first, the second stays second, and so on, unless you explicitly change the order.

- **Indexed**: Each item (or **element**) in an array has a numeric position called an **index**. Importantly, array indexes in JavaScript are **zero-based**, meaning the first element is at index 0, the second at index 1, the third at index 2, and so forth.
- **Flexible**: Arrays can hold elements of any data type – numbers, strings, booleans, other objects, even other arrays! You can mix different types within the same array.
- **Dynamic**: JavaScript arrays can grow or shrink in size as needed; you can add or remove elements after the array is created.

Imagine a list of tasks for the day:

1. Wake up
2. Make coffee
3. Check email
4. Code!

In an array, this would look like:

- Index 0: "Wake up"
- Index 1: "Make coffee"
- Index 2: "Check email"
- Index 3: "Code!"

Creating Arrays

The most common and preferred way to create an array in JavaScript is using **array literal** syntax, which involves enclosing a comma-separated list of elements within square brackets [].

```
// An empty array
let emptyList = [];
console.log(emptyList); // *Output: []*

// An array of strings (programming languages)
let languages = ["JavaScript", "Python", "Java", "C++"];
console.log(languages); // *Output: [ 'JavaScript', 'Python', 'Java', 'C++' ]*

// An array of numbers (scores)
let highScores = [98, 95, 92, 88, 85];
console.log(highScores); // *Output: [ 98, 95, 92, 88, 85 ]*

// An array with mixed data types
```

```
let mixedData = ["Alice", 30, true, null, { theme: "dark" }];
// *Contains string, number, boolean, null, and an object (Chapter 7)*
console.log(mixedData); // *Output: [ 'Alice', 30, true, null, { theme: 'dark' }
]*

// An array containing another array (nested array or multi-dimensional)
let matrix = [
  [1, 2, 3],
  [4, 5, 6],
  [7, 8, 9]
];
console.log(matrix); // *Output: [ [ 1, 2, 3 ], [ 4, 5, 6 ], [ 7, 8, 9 ] ]*
```

Note on new Array(): You might occasionally see arrays created using new Array(). While this works, it can sometimes be confusing (e.g., new Array(5) creates an empty array with length 5, but new Array(5, 10) creates an array [5, 10]). For clarity and consistency, **stick with the array literal [] syntax.**

Accessing Array Elements (Indexes)

To retrieve an element from an array, you use square bracket notation [] immediately following the array variable name, placing the **zero-based index** of the desired element inside the brackets.

```
let fruits = ["Apple", "Banana", "Cherry", "Date"];

// Access the first element (index 0)
let firstFruit = fruits[0];
console.log(firstFruit); // *Output: Apple*

// Access the third element (index 2)
let thirdFruit = fruits[2];
console.log(thirdFruit); // *Output: Cherry*

// Access the last element
// (Length is 4, so last index is 4 - 1 = 3)
let lastFruit = fruits[fruits.length - 1];
console.log(lastFruit); // *Output: Date*

// What happens if the index is out of bounds?
let nonExistent = fruits[10];
console.log(nonExistent); // *Output: undefined*
```

Trying to access an index that doesn't exist in the array doesn't cause an error; it simply returns the value undefined, which we learned about in Chapter 2.

Modifying Array Elements

You can change the value of an element at a specific index using assignment (=), just like with regular variables, but using the bracket notation to specify the target element.

```
let colors = ["Red", "Green", "Blue"];
console.log("Original colors:", colors); // *Output: Original colors: [ 'Red',
'Green', 'Blue' ]*

// Change the element at index 1 (Green) to 'Yellow'
colors[1] = "Yellow";
console.log("Modified colors:", colors); // *Output: Modified colors: [ 'Red',
'Yellow', 'Blue' ]*

// You can even add elements by assigning to a new index
colors[3] = "Purple"; // *Adds 'Purple' at index 3*
console.log("Added color:", colors); // *Output: Added color: [ 'Red', 'Yellow',
'Blue', 'Purple' ]*
```

Array Properties: length

Every array has a built-in length property that tells you how many elements are currently in the array. This property is incredibly useful, especially when you need to loop through all the elements.

```
let tools = ["Hammer", "Screwdriver", "Wrench"];
console.log(tools.length); // *Output: 3*

let numbers = [10, 20, 30, 40, 50, 60];
console.log(numbers.length); // *Output: 6*

let empty = [];
console.log(empty.length); // *Output: 0*

// The length property updates automatically when you add/remove elements
tools.push("Pliers"); // *Add an element (more on push() soon)*
console.log(tools);        // *Output: [ 'Hammer', 'Screwdriver', 'Wrench',
'Pliers' ]*
```

```
console.log(tools.length); // *Output: 4*
```

As seen in the `fruits` example earlier, `array.length - 1` is a reliable way to get the index of the *last* element in any non-empty array.

Common Array Methods

Arrays come equipped with many built-in **methods**. Methods are essentially functions associated with an object (in this case, the array) that perform actions on or related to that object. You call a method using dot notation (`.`) followed by the method name and parentheses (`)`. Some methods require arguments inside the parentheses.

Let's explore some of the most frequently used array methods:

Adding/Removing Elements

These methods modify the original array (they are "mutating" or "destructive").

- `push(item1, item2, ...)`: Adds one or more elements to the **end** of the array. It returns the new `length` of the array.

  ```
  let planets = ["Mercury", "Venus", "Earth"];
  let newLength = planets.push("Mars", "Jupiter");

  console.log(planets);    // *Output: [ 'Mercury', 'Venus', 'Earth',
  'Mars', 'Jupiter' ]*
  console.log(newLength); // *Output: 5*
  ```

- `pop()`: Removes the **last** element from the array. It returns the element that was removed.

  ```
  let browsers = ["Chrome", "Firefox", "Safari", "Edge"];
  let removedBrowser = browsers.pop();

  console.log(browsers);      // *Output: [ 'Chrome', 'Firefox',
  'Safari' ]*
  console.log(removedBrowser);// *Output: Edge*
  ```

- `unshift(item1, item2, ...)`: Adds one or more elements to the **beginning** of the array. It returns the new `length` of the array. (Note: Can be less efficient than `push` for very large arrays as all existing elements need to be re-indexed).

```
let letters = ["C", "D"];
let newLength2 = letters.unshift("A", "B");

console.log(letters);     // *Output: [ 'A', 'B', 'C', 'D' ]*
console.log(newLength2); // *Output: 4*
```

- shift(): Removes the **first** element from the array. It returns the element that was removed. (Like unshift, this can be less efficient for large arrays).

```
let queue = ["First", "Second", "Third"];
let nextInLine = queue.shift();

console.log(queue);       // *Output: [ 'Second', 'Third' ]*
console.log(nextInLine); // *Output: First*
```

Slicing and Splicing

These methods deal with portions of the array.

- slice(startIndex, endIndex): Returns a **new** array containing a shallow copy of a portion of the original array, from startIndex (inclusive) up to endIndex (exclusive). **It does not modify the original array.**

    - If endIndex is omitted, it slices to the end of the array.
    - If startIndex is omitted (or 0), it slices from the beginning.
    - Negative indexes can be used to count from the end (-1 is the last element, -2 is the second-to-last, etc.).

```
let animals = ["Ant", "Bison", "Camel", "Duck", "Elephant"];

// Get elements from index 2 ('Camel') up to (not including) index 4
('Elephant')
let middleAnimals = animals.slice(2, 4);
console.log(middleAnimals); // *Output: [ 'Camel', 'Duck' ]*

// Get elements from index 1 ('Bison') to the end
let allButFirst = animals.slice(1);
console.log(allButFirst); // *Output: [ 'Bison', 'Camel', 'Duck',
'Elephant' ]*

// Get the last two elements
let lastTwo = animals.slice(-2);
console.log(lastTwo); // *Output: [ 'Duck', 'Elephant' ]*
```

```
// Create a copy of the whole array
let animalsCopy = animals.slice();
console.log(animalsCopy); // *Output: [ 'Ant', 'Bison', 'Camel', 'Duck',
'Elephant' ]*

console.log("Original array is unchanged:", animals);
// *Output: Original array is unchanged: [ 'Ant', 'Bison', 'Camel',
'Duck', 'Elephant' ]*
```

- splice(startIndex, deleteCount, item1, item2, ...): **Changes the original array** by removing, replacing, or adding elements. It returns an array containing the elements that were deleted (if any).

    - startIndex: The index at which to start changing the array.
    - deleteCount: The number of elements to remove (starting from startIndex).
    - item1, item2, ... (optional): Elements to add to the array at startIndex after removing elements.

```
let months = ["Jan", "March", "April", "June"];
console.log("Original:", months); // *Output: Original: [ 'Jan',
'March', 'April', 'June' ]*

// Insert 'Feb' at index 1
// Start at index 1, delete 0 elements, add 'Feb'
let deleted1 = months.splice(1, 0, "Feb");
console.log("After insert:", months);   // *Output: After insert:
[ 'Jan', 'Feb', 'March', 'April', 'June' ]*
console.log("Deleted:", deleted1); // *Output: Deleted: []*

// Replace 'April' with 'May'
// Start at index 3 ('April'), delete 1 element, add 'May'
let deleted2 = months.splice(3, 1, "May");
console.log("After replace:", months);   // *Output: After replace:
[ 'Jan', 'Feb', 'March', 'May', 'June' ]*
console.log("Deleted:", deleted2); // *Output: Deleted: [ 'April' ]*

// Remove 'June' (index 4)
// Start at index 4, delete 1 element
let deleted3 = months.splice(4, 1);
console.log("After remove:", months);   // *Output: After remove:
[ 'Jan', 'Feb', 'March', 'May' ]*
console.log("Deleted:", deleted3); // *Output: Deleted: [ 'June' ]*
```

Because `splice` modifies the original array, use it carefully. Use `slice` when you need a portion without changing the source.

Finding Elements

- `indexOf(searchElement, fromIndex)`: Searches the array for `searchElement` and returns the **first index** at which it is found. If the element is not found, it returns `-1`.

    - `fromIndex` (optional): The index to start the search from.

    ```
    let tools = ["Hammer", "Wrench", "Screwdriver", "Wrench"];

    console.log(tools.indexOf("Wrench")); // *Output: 1 (finds the first
    'Wrench')*
    console.log(tools.indexOf("Pliers")); // *Output: -1 (not found)*

    // Find 'Wrench' starting search from index 2
    console.log(tools.indexOf("Wrench", 2)); // *Output: 3*
    ```

- `includes(searchElement, fromIndex)`: Checks if an array includes `searchElement`, returning `true` or `false`. This is often simpler and clearer than checking if `indexOf` returns `-1`.

    - `fromIndex` (optional): The index to start the search from.

    ```
    let pets = ["cat", "dog", "rabbit"];

    console.log(pets.includes("dog"));    // *Output: true*
    console.log(pets.includes("fish"));   // *Output: false*

    // Check for 'cat' starting from index 1
    console.log(pets.includes("cat", 1)); // *Output: false*
    ```

There are many more array methods available (like `map`, `filter`, `reduce`, `sort`, etc.), which enable powerful data transformations. We'll encounter some of these in later chapters as we explore more advanced concepts, particularly functional programming patterns.

Iterating Over Arrays with Loops

As previewed in Chapter 5, loops are essential for processing each element in an array.

The Standard `for` Loop

This classic approach gives you access to both the index (`i`) and the element (`array[i]`).

```
let scores = [85, 92, 78, 99];
let total = 0;

for (let i = 0; i < scores.length; i++) {
  console.log(`Processing score at index ${i}: ${scores[i]}`);
  total += scores[i]; // *Add current score to total*
}

let average = total / scores.length;
console.log(`Total score: ${total}`);       // *Output: Total score: 354*
console.log(`Average score: ${average}`); // *Output: Average score: 88.5*
```

The `for...of` Loop

If you only need the **value** of each element and not its index, the `for...of` loop (introduced in ES6) provides a cleaner syntax:

```
let names = ["Alice", "Bob", "Charlie"];

console.log("Guest list:");
for (let name of names) {
  // 'name' directly holds the element value in each iteration
  console.log(`- Welcome, ${name}!`);
}

// *Output:*
// Guest list:
// - Welcome, Alice!
// - Welcome, Bob!
// - Welcome, Charlie!
```

The `forEach` Method

Arrays also have a `forEach` method that executes a provided function once for each array element. This uses a "callback" function, a concept we'll explore more thoroughly when we dive deeper into functions (Chapter 8).

```
let groceries = ["Milk", "Bread", "Eggs"];

console.log("Shopping list:");
groceries.forEach(function(item, index) {
  // *The function receives the item and its index*
  console.log(`Item ${index + 1}: ${item}`);
});

// *Output:*
// Shopping list:
// Item 1: Milk
// Item 2: Bread
// Item 3: Eggs
```

For now, the standard `for` loop and the `for...of` loop are excellent tools for array iteration.

Chapter Summary

In this chapter, we learned about **Arrays**, JavaScript's fundamental structure for storing ordered collections of data. We saw how to create arrays using **array literals** [] and how to access and modify their elements using **zero-based indexes** with bracket notation `arrayName[index]`. We explored the dynamic `length` property, which tells us the size of the array. We then delved into essential **array methods** for manipulating arrays: adding/removing elements (`push`, `pop`, `unshift`, `shift`), getting portions (`slice`), modifying in place (`splice`), and finding elements (`indexOf`, `includes`). Finally, we revisited how to process array elements using loops, highlighting the standard `for` **loop**, the convenient `for...of` **loop**, and the `forEach` method.

Arrays are perfect for ordered lists where the position (index) matters. However, sometimes we need to store data where items are identified by descriptive labels rather than numerical positions, like storing properties of a user (name, email, age). For this, JavaScript offers another crucial data structure: **Objects**. In the next chapter, we'll explore objects and how they allow us to represent more complex, structured data using key-value pairs.

7

Objects

In the last chapter, we explored arrays – JavaScript's way of storing ordered lists of items, like a grocery list or a sequence of steps. We accessed items using their numerical position, or index. Arrays are fantastic when the order matters and you just need a list. But what if you need to represent something with more structure, where each piece of data has a specific label or description?

Think about describing a car. You wouldn't just list its attributes like ["Red", 2022, "Sedan", "Toyota"]. It's much clearer to label each piece: Color is "Red", Year is 2022, Type is "Sedan", Make is "Toyota". This labeled structure is exactly what **Objects** provide in JavaScript. While arrays are like ordered, numbered lists, objects are more like dictionaries or file cabinets, where you store information under specific named labels (keys).

What is an Object?

In JavaScript, an object is a collection of related data and/or functionality. Unlike arrays which use numerical indexes, objects store data in **key-value pairs**. These pairs are often called **properties**.

- **Key:** A string (or, less commonly for beginners, a Symbol) that acts as the unique identifier for a value within the object. Think of it as the label on a container or a word in a dictionary.

- **Value:** The actual data associated with the key. This can be *any* JavaScript data type – a string, number, boolean, array, even another object!

Key characteristics of objects:

- **Unordered (Historically):** Traditionally, the order of properties in a JavaScript object wasn't guaranteed. While modern JavaScript has made property order more predictable in many situations (especially for non-integer keys), you generally shouldn't rely on a specific order when working with object properties, unlike arrays where order is fundamental.
- **Key-Based Access:** You access values using their corresponding keys, not numerical indexes.
- **Modeling:** Objects are perfect for modeling real-world things (like a user, a product, a configuration) or abstract concepts that have distinct properties.

Creating Objects

Just like arrays have a literal syntax (`[]`), objects have one too, which is the most common and recommended way to create them: **object literal** syntax, using curly braces `{}`.

Inside the curly braces, you define the properties as `key: value` pairs, separated by commas.

```
// An empty object
let emptyObject = {};
console.log(emptyObject); // *Output: {}*

// An object representing a user
let user = {
  firstName: "Grace", // *'firstName' is the key, "Grace" is the value*
  lastName: "Hopper",
  occupation: "Computer Scientist",
  isAdmin: true,
  logins: 99
};
console.log(user);
// *Output: { firstName: 'Grace', lastName: 'Hopper',
// *          occupation: 'Computer Scientist', isAdmin: true, logins: 99 }*

// An object representing a book
let book = {
  title: "Eloquent JavaScript",
  author: "Marijn Haverbeke",
```

```
  "publication year": 2018, // *Key with space needs quotes*
  genres: ["Programming", "Web Development", "JavaScript"], // *Value is an
array*
  isAvailable: true
};
console.log(book);
/* Output:
{
  title: 'Eloquent JavaScript',
  author: 'Marijn Haverbeke',
  'publication year': 2018,
  genres: [ 'Programming', 'Web Development', 'JavaScript' ],
  isAvailable: true
}
*/
```

Key Naming:

- If the key is a valid JavaScript identifier (starts with a letter, _, or $, and contains only letters, numbers, _, or $), you can write it directly without quotes (like firstName). This is the preferred style when possible.
- If the key contains spaces, special characters, or starts with a number, you **must** enclose it in quotes (single or double), like "publication year".

Accessing Object Properties

Once you have an object, you need a way to retrieve the values stored within it. JavaScript offers two primary ways to access object properties:

Dot Notation

This is the most common and often preferred method when the property key is a valid identifier. You simply use the object variable name followed by a dot (.) and then the property key.

```
let spaceship = {
  name: "Millennium Falcon",
  pilot: "Han Solo",
  maxSpeed: "105 MGLT",
  cargoCapacity: 100000 // *in kg*
};

// Accessing properties using dot notation
```

```
let shipName = spaceship.name;
let pilotName = spaceship.pilot;

console.log(`Ship: ${shipName}`);     // *Output: Ship: Millennium Falcon*
console.log(`Pilot: ${pilotName}`); // *Output: Pilot: Han Solo*

// You can use dot notation in expressions too
let speedDescription = `Max speed is ${spaceship.maxSpeed}`;
console.log(speedDescription); // *Output: Max speed is 105 MGLT*
```

Dot notation is concise and generally easy to read.

Bracket Notation

The second way to access properties is using square brackets [], similar to how you access array elements. However, instead of a numerical index, you place the **key** (usually as a string) inside the brackets.

```
let product = {
  id: "XYZ-123",
  "product name": "Wireless Mouse", // *Key with space*
  price: 25.99,
  inStock: true
};

// Accessing using bracket notation
let productId = product['id'];
console.log(`Product ID: ${productId}`); // *Output: Product ID: XYZ-123*

// Bracket notation is REQUIRED for keys that are not valid identifiers
let productName = product['product name'];
console.log(`Name: ${productName}`); // *Output: Name: Wireless Mouse*
// *product."product name" would cause a syntax error*

// You can also use a variable containing the key name
let keyToAccess = "price";
let productPrice = product[keyToAccess]; // *Access using the variable*
console.log(`Price: $${productPrice}`); // *Output: Price: $25.99*
```

When to use Bracket Notation:

1. When the property key has spaces, special characters, or starts with a number (i.e., it's not a valid identifier).

2. When the property key is stored in a variable or determined dynamically at runtime.

If the key is a simple, valid identifier, dot notation is generally preferred for its cleaner look.

Accessing Non-existent Properties: Just like with arrays, trying to access a property that doesn't exist on an object results in undefined, not an error.

```
let person = { name: "Alice", age: 30 };
console.log(person.email); // *Output: undefined*
```

Modifying Object Properties

You can easily change the value associated with an existing key using either dot or bracket notation combined with the assignment operator (=).

```
let settings = {
  theme: "light",
  fontSize: 14,
  notificationsEnabled: true
};
console.log("Initial settings:", settings);
/* Output:
Initial settings: { theme: 'light', fontSize: 14, notificationsEnabled: true }
*/

// Modify using dot notation
settings.theme = "dark";

// Modify using bracket notation
settings['fontSize'] = 16;

console.log("Updated settings:", settings);
/* Output:
Updated settings: { theme: 'dark', fontSize: 16, notificationsEnabled: true }
*/
```

Adding and Deleting Properties

Objects are dynamic; you can add new properties or remove existing ones after the object has been created.

Adding Properties

To add a new property, simply assign a value to a new key using either dot or bracket notation. If the key doesn't exist, JavaScript will create it for you.

```
let character = {
  name: "Frodo",
  race: "Hobbit"
};
console.log("Before adding:", character);
// *Output: Before adding: { name: 'Frodo', race: 'Hobbit' }*

// Add properties using dot notation
character.hasRing = true;

// Add properties using bracket notation
character["home town"] = "The Shire";

console.log("After adding:", character);
/* Output:
After adding: {
  name: 'Frodo',
  race: 'Hobbit',
  hasRing: true,
  'home town': 'The Shire'
}
*/
```

Deleting Properties

To completely remove a property (both the key and its value) from an object, you use the `delete` operator.

```
let course = {
  title: "Intro to JS",
  duration: "10 weeks",
  instructor: "Dr. Script",
  platform: "Online"
};
console.log("Before delete:", course);
/* Output:
Before delete: {
  title: 'Intro to JS',
  duration: '10 weeks',
  instructor: 'Dr. Script',
```

```
    platform: 'Online'
}
*/

// Delete the 'platform' property
delete course.platform;
// *You could also use: delete course['platform'];*

console.log("After delete:", course);
/* Output:
After delete: {
  title: 'Intro to JS',
  duration: '10 weeks',
  instructor: 'Dr. Script'
}
*/

console.log(course.platform); // *Output: undefined*
```

The `delete` operator returns `true` if the deletion was successful (or if the property didn't exist) and `false` if the property cannot be deleted (which is rare for simple object properties). While functional, excessive use of `delete` can sometimes impact performance in highly optimized scenarios, but for most common uses, it's perfectly fine.

Objects Can Hold Anything (Even Functions!)

The values associated with keys in an object aren't limited to simple primitives like strings or numbers. They can hold complex data structures too.

```
let project = {
  projectName: "Website Redesign",
  status: "In Progress",
  dueDate: "2024-12-31",
  teamMembers: ["Alice", "Bob", "Charlie"], // *Array as a value*
  client: { // *Another object as a value (nested object)*
    name: "Acme Corp",
    contactPerson: "Diana Prince"
  }
};

// Accessing nested data
console.log(project.projectName); // *Output: Website Redesign*
console.log(project.teamMembers[1]); // *Access array element: Output: Bob*
```

```
console.log(project.client.contactPerson); // *Access nested object property:
Output: Diana Prince*
```

Methods

One of the most powerful features of objects is that their property values can be **functions**. When a function is stored as a property of an object, it's called a **method**. Methods define behaviors or actions that the object can perform, often operating on the object's own data.

```
let calculator = {
  operand1: 0,
  operand2: 0,

  // Method to set the operands
  setOperands: function(num1, num2) {
    this.operand1 = num1;
    this.operand2 = num2;
    console.log(`Operands set to ${num1} and ${num2}`);
  },

  // Method to perform addition
  add: function() {
    let result = this.operand1 + this.operand2;
    console.log(`Addition Result: ${result}`);
    return result;
  },

  // Method to perform subtraction
  subtract: function() {
    let result = this.operand1 - this.operand2;
     console.log(`Subtraction Result: ${result}`);
    return result;
  }
};

// Call the methods using dot notation
calculator.setOperands(10, 5); // *Output: Operands set to 10 and 5*
calculator.add();              // *Output: Addition Result: 15*
calculator.subtract();         // *Output: Subtraction Result: 5*
```

Notice how methods are defined just like regular function expressions (which we'll formally cover in Chapter 8) assigned to a key. You call them using dot notation followed by parentheses (), just like a regular function call.

A First Look at `this`

Inside the `calculator` methods, you saw the keyword `this` (`this.operand1`, `this.operand2`). What does `this` mean?

In the context of an object method called using dot notation (like `calculator.add()`), `this` typically refers to **the object itself** – the object the method was called on. So, inside `add()`, `this` refers to the `calculator` object. This allows the `add` method to access other properties of the *same object*, like `operand1` and `operand2`.

Without `this`, the `add` function wouldn't inherently know which `operand1` or `operand2` to use if there were multiple calculators or variables with those names elsewhere. `this` provides context, linking the method's execution to the specific object instance.

The behavior of `this` is actually one of the more complex topics in JavaScript and depends heavily on *how* a function is called. We'll revisit it in more detail later, but for now, understand that within a method called like `object.method()`, `this` usually points to `object`.

Chapter Summary

This chapter introduced **Objects**, JavaScript's way of storing structured data using **key-value pairs** (properties). We learned the primary way to create them using **object literal syntax** `{}`. We explored the two ways to access and modify properties: **dot notation** (`object.property`) for valid identifiers and **bracket notation** (`object['property']`) for keys with special characters or when using variables. We saw how to dynamically **add** properties by assignment and **remove** them using the `delete` operator. Crucially, we learned that object values can be any data type, including other objects (nesting) and functions. When functions are stored as properties, they become **methods**, defining the object's behavior. We also had our first encounter with the `this` keyword within methods, understanding its role in providing context and allowing methods to access their object's own properties.

Objects and arrays are the primary ways you'll organize data in JavaScript. Now that we've seen how functions can be stored *inside* objects as methods, it's time to take a much deeper look at functions themselves. In the next chapter, we'll explore how to define and use **Functions** as reusable blocks of code, understanding parameters, return values, and scope – concepts essential for writing organized, modular, and efficient JavaScript programs.

8

Functions

In the previous chapter, we explored objects and saw how they can contain not just data (properties) but also actions (methods, which are functions stored as properties). This idea of packaging code that performs a specific task is incredibly powerful and fundamental to programming. Imagine you need to calculate the area of a rectangle multiple times in your program with different dimensions, or format a user's name consistently across various parts of your application. Copying and pasting the same logic everywhere would be inefficient and a nightmare to update if the logic needed to change.

This chapter dives deep into **Functions**, the primary mechanism in JavaScript for creating reusable, named blocks of code. Think of functions like mini-programs within your larger program, or like specialized tools in a workshop – you define the tool once (like a recipe) and then use it whenever you need that specific job done. Mastering functions is essential for writing organized, maintainable, and non-repetitive code.

Why Use Functions? The DRY Principle

As mentioned, the core reason to use functions is to avoid repeating yourself. This aligns with the **DRY (Don't Repeat Yourself)** principle, a cornerstone of good software development. But the benefits go beyond just avoiding repetition:

- **Reusability:** Define a piece of logic once and call it from multiple places in your code.
- **Organization:** Break down complex programs into smaller, manageable, logical units. Each function handles a specific task, making the overall structure clearer.
- **Readability:** Give descriptive names to blocks of code, making it easier to understand what the code does without needing to read every line of the implementation. For example, `calculateTotalPrice()` is more immediately understandable than several lines of arithmetic operations.
- **Maintainability:** If you need to fix a bug or update the logic for a specific task, you only need to change it inside the corresponding function definition. The change automatically applies everywhere the function is called.
- **Abstraction:** Functions hide the complexity of *how* a task is done. When you call a function, you only need to know *what* it does (and what inputs it needs), not necessarily the intricate details of its internal workings.

Defining Functions

Before you can use (or "call") a function, you need to define it. JavaScript provides two main ways to define functions: function declarations and function expressions.

Function Declarations

This is often considered the "classic" way to define a function. It starts with the `function` keyword, followed by the function's name, a list of parameters in parentheses `()`, and the code block (function body) enclosed in curly braces `{}`.

```
// Function declaration syntax
function greetUser(name) {
  // 'name' is a parameter
  let message = `Hello, ${name}! Welcome.`;
  console.log(message);
}

function calculateRectangleArea(width, height) {
  // 'width' and 'height' are parameters
  let area = width * height;
  return area; // *Returns the calculated value*
}
```

- `function` **keyword:** Signals the start of a function definition.

- **Function Name** (`greetUser`, `calculateRectangleArea`): A descriptive name following standard variable naming conventions (camelCase is common). This name is used to call the function later.
- **Parameters** (`name`, `width`, `height`): Variables listed inside the parentheses. They act as placeholders for the input values (arguments) that the function will receive when it's called. A function can have zero or more parameters, separated by commas.
- **Function Body** (`{...}`): The block of code containing the statements that perform the function's task. Variables declared inside the function body (like `message` and `area` above) are typically local to that function (more on scope later).
- `return` **statement (optional)**: Specifies the value that the function should output back to the code that called it. We'll discuss `return` in detail shortly.

One key characteristic of function declarations is **hoisting**. JavaScript conceptually moves function *declarations* (but not function *expressions*) to the top of their scope before code execution. This means you can technically call a function declared this way *before* its actual definition appears in the code (though structuring code with definitions first is generally better for readability). We'll revisit hoisting in Chapter 9.

Function Expressions

Another way to define a function is by creating a function and assigning it to a variable. This is called a function expression.

```
// Function expression syntax
let sayGoodbye = function(name) {
  console.log(`Goodbye, ${name}!`);
}; // *Note the semicolon here, as it's part of an assignment statement*

const findSquare = function(number) {
  return number * number;
};
```

Here, the function itself doesn't necessarily have a name right after the `function` keyword (making it an **anonymous function**). Instead, the variable (`sayGoodbye`, `findSquare`) holds a reference to the function, and you use that variable name to call it.

- `let/const/var`: You use standard variable declaration keywords.
- **Variable Name** (`sayGoodbye`, `findSquare`): This is how you'll refer to the function.

- =: The assignment operator.
- `function(...) {...}`: The function definition itself (often anonymous).

Function expressions are **not hoisted** in the same way as declarations. While the variable declaration (`let sayGoodbye;`) might be hoisted (depending on `let/const/var`), the function *assignment* only happens when the execution reaches that line. This means you **cannot** call a function defined via an expression *before* the line where it's defined.

Declaration vs. Expression - Which to Use? Both are valid and widely used.

- Declarations are often simpler for straightforward named functions and benefit from hoisting (which can sometimes be helpful, sometimes confusing).
- Expressions are powerful, allowing functions to be treated like any other value – assigned to variables, passed as arguments to other functions, etc. They are essential for concepts like callbacks and closures (which we'll touch upon later).
- Many modern JavaScript developers lean towards using function expressions (especially with `const`) or the newer Arrow Function syntax (covered in Chapter 18) as they can offer clearer scoping behavior with `let` and `const`.

For now, understand both forms exist and how their basic definition differs.

Calling (Invoking) Functions

Defining a function doesn't execute its code. It just creates the recipe. To actually run the code inside the function body, you need to **call** (or **invoke**) the function. You do this by using the function's name (or the variable name holding the function expression) followed by parentheses ().

```
// Define the functions (using declarations here)
function displayGreeting() {
  console.log("Hello there!");
}

function addNumbers(num1, num2) {
  let sum = num1 + num2;
  console.log(`The sum is: ${sum}`);
}

// Call the functions
displayGreeting(); // *Executes the code inside displayGreeting*
addNumbers(5, 7);  // *Executes addNumbers, passing 5 and 7 as arguments*
```

```
// *Output:*
// Hello there!
// The sum is: 12
```

When you call a function, the program's execution jumps from the calling point into the function's body, executes the statements inside, and then (usually) returns to the point right after where the function was called.

Parameters and Arguments

Functions become much more versatile when you can pass information *into* them.

- **Parameters:** These are the variables listed in the function definition's parentheses (function funcName(param1, param2) {...}). They act as named placeholders within the function, waiting to receive values.
- **Arguments:** These are the actual values you provide when you *call* the function (funcName(arg1, arg2)).

When you call a function, the arguments you pass are assigned to the corresponding parameters based on their order.

```
function introducePet(petType, petName) {
  // 'petType' and 'petName' are parameters
  console.log(`I have a ${petType} named ${petName}.`);
}

// Call the function with arguments
introducePet("cat", "Whiskers"); // *"cat" is assigned to petType, "Whiskers" to
petName*
introducePet("dog", "Buddy");    // *"dog" is assigned to petType, "Buddy" to
petName*

// *Output:*
// I have a cat named Whiskers.
// I have a dog named Buddy.
```

What happens if the number of arguments doesn't match the number of parameters?

- **Too Few Arguments:** If you pass fewer arguments than parameters, the parameters that don't receive an argument are assigned the default value undefined.

70

```
function showDetails(name, age) {
  console.log(`Name: ${name}, Age: ${age}`);
}
showDetails("Alice"); // *'age' parameter receives no argument*
// *Output: Name: Alice, Age: undefined*
```

- **Too Many Arguments:** If you pass more arguments than parameters, the extra arguments are generally ignored (though they are accessible via a special arguments object inside the function, which is less commonly used in modern JS).

```
function showDetails(name, age) {
  console.log(`Name: ${name}, Age: ${age}`);
}
showDetails("Bob", 35, "Engineer"); // *"Engineer" argument is ignored*
// *Output: Name: Bob, Age: 35*
```

Returning Values

Many functions perform a calculation or task and need to send a result *back* to the code that called them. This is done using the return statement.

When a return statement is executed inside a function:

1. The function immediately stops executing (even if there's more code after the return).
2. The value specified after the return keyword is sent back as the result of the function call.

```
function multiply(num1, num2) {
  let product = num1 * num2;
  return product; // *Send the calculated product back*

  // *Code here would never run because it's after return*
  // console.log("Calculation complete!");
}

function formatUserName(first, last) {
    if (!first || !last) {
        return "Invalid name provided"; // *Return early if input is bad*
    }
    return `${last}, ${first}`; // *Return the formatted string*
```

```
}

// Call the functions and store their return values
let result = multiply(6, 7);
console.log(result); // *Output: 42*

let formattedName1 = formatUserName("Brendan", "Eich");
console.log(formattedName1); // *Output: Eich, Brendan*

let formattedName2 = formatUserName("Ada"); // *Missing last name*
console.log(formattedName2); // *Output: Invalid name provided*
```

What if a function doesn't have a `return` **statement, or just** `return;`? If a function reaches its end without executing a `return` statement that specifies a value, it implicitly returns `undefined`.

```
function logMessage(message) {
  console.log(message);
  // *No explicit return statement*
}

let returnValue = logMessage("Testing return value"); // *Logs "Testing return
value"*
console.log(returnValue); // *Output: undefined*
```

So, functions that are primarily used for performing an action (like logging to the console or modifying the DOM) might not have an explicit `return` statement, implicitly returning `undefined`. Functions designed to compute a value *must* use `return` to make that value available.

Default Parameters

Before ES6, handling cases where arguments might not be passed often involved checking if a parameter was `undefined` inside the function and assigning a default value manually. Modern JavaScript (ES6+) makes this much easier with **default parameters**.

You can specify a default value directly in the parameter list using the assignment operator (=). If an argument is not provided for that parameter during the function call (or if `undefined` is explicitly passed), the default value will be used instead.

```
function greet(name = "Guest", greeting = "Hello") {
```

```
    // *'Guest' is the default for name, 'Hello' for greeting*
    console.log(`${greeting}, ${name}!`);
}

greet("Alice", "Hi"); // *Output: Hi, Alice!*
greet("Bob");          // *Uses default greeting: Output: Hello, Bob!*
greet(undefined, "Good morning"); // *Uses default name: Output: Good morning,
Guest!*
greet();               // *Uses both defaults: Output: Hello, Guest!*
```

Default parameters make function definitions cleaner and more robust when dealing with optional arguments.

Understanding Function Scope (Introduction)

Where can variables declared inside a function be accessed? This relates to the concept of **scope**, which defines the visibility and accessibility of variables.

A fundamental rule is: **Variables declared inside a function (using** `let`, `const`, **or** `var`) **are generally local to that function.** They cannot be accessed from outside the function.

```
function calculate() {
  let localVar = 100; // *Local variable*
  const constantVar = 200;
  console.log(`Inside function: ${localVar}, ${constantVar}`);
}

calculate(); // *Output: Inside function: 100, 200*

// *Trying to access local variables outside the function will cause an error:*
// console.log(localVar); // *ReferenceError: localVar is not defined*
// console.log(constantVar); // *ReferenceError: constantVar is not defined*
```

This local scope is crucial. It prevents variable names used inside one function from accidentally interfering with variables of the same name used elsewhere in your program. Each function creates its own private workspace.

Conversely, functions *can* typically access variables declared in their **outer scope** (the environment where the function was defined). This is called **lexical scoping**.

```
let globalMessage = "I'm global!";
```

```
function showMessages() {
  let localMessage = "I'm local!";
  console.log(localMessage);  // *Accesses its own local variable*
  console.log(globalMessage); // *Accesses the variable from the outer (global)
scope*
}

showMessages();
// *Output:*
// I'm local!
// I'm global!
```

Scope is a critical concept for understanding how variables behave in JavaScript, especially with nested functions and closures. We've only scratched the surface here. **Chapter 9 will be dedicated entirely to exploring Scope and Hoisting in much greater detail.**

Chapter Summary

This chapter focused on **Functions**, the building blocks for creating reusable and organized code in JavaScript. We established *why* functions are essential, emphasizing the **DRY principle** and benefits like reusability, organization, and maintainability. We learned the two main ways to define functions: **function declarations** (which are hoisted) and **function expressions** (assigned to variables, not hoisted). We saw how to **call** functions using parentheses () and how to pass data into them using **parameters** (in the definition) and **arguments** (in the call). The crucial role of the return statement for sending values *out* of functions was explained, along with the concept of functions implicitly returning undefined. We also explored modern **default parameters** for handling optional arguments cleanly. Finally, we had an introductory look at **function scope**, establishing that variables declared inside functions are typically local, while functions can access variables from their outer scopes.

You now understand how to define and use functions to structure your code effectively. However, the brief introduction to scope hinted at more complex interactions between functions and variables. In the next chapter, we will dive deep into the rules governing **Scope and Hoisting** in JavaScript, clarifying exactly where variables and functions live and how JavaScript processes their declarations. This knowledge is vital for preventing bugs and writing predictable code.

9

Scope and Hoisting

In Chapter 8, we learned how to create reusable blocks of code with functions. We saw that variables declared inside a function are generally local to that function. But how exactly does JavaScript know which variables are accessible where? Why can a function sometimes use variables defined outside of it? And have you ever wondered if it matters *where* in your code you declare a variable or a function?

These questions revolve around two fundamental concepts in JavaScript: **Scope** and **Hoisting**. Scope determines the visibility and accessibility of variables and functions in different parts of your code. Hoisting describes how JavaScript handles declarations *before* the code is actually executed. Understanding these concepts is not just academic; it's crucial for writing correct, predictable, and bug-free JavaScript code. Misunderstanding scope and hoisting is a common source of errors, especially for beginners. Let's unravel these mysteries.

What is Scope?

Think of scope as the set of rules that determines where variables, functions, and objects are accessible within your running code. It's like the visibility rules in a building: someone in the lobby (global scope) might be visible to many, while someone inside a private office (function scope) is only visible within that office, and someone in a specific meeting room within that office (block scope) might only be visible there.

Scope defines the "lifespan" and accessibility of variables. It prevents variables in different parts of your program from colliding or interfering with each other if they happen to share the same name. There are different types of scope in JavaScript, primarily:

1. **Global Scope**
2. **Function Scope**
3. **Block Scope**

Let's look at each one.

Global Scope

Any variable or function declared *outside* of any function or block ({}) resides in the **global scope**. Variables in the global scope are accessible from *anywhere* in your JavaScript code – inside functions, inside blocks, everywhere.

```javascript
// 'appName' is in the global scope
let appName = "My Awesome App";
const appVersion = "1.0";

function displayAppInfo() {
  console.log(`Running ${appName}, version ${appVersion}`); // *Can access
globals*

  // 'platform' is local to this function (Function Scope)
  let platform = "Web Browser";
  console.log(`Platform: ${platform}`);
}

if (true) {
  // 'isSupported' is local to this block (Block Scope if using let/const)
  let isSupported = true;
  console.log(`Is ${appName} supported? ${isSupported}`); // *Can access global*
}

displayAppInfo();
// *console.log(platform); // Error! platform is not defined globally*
// *console.log(isSupported); // Error! isSupported is not defined globally*
```

In a browser environment, global variables declared with var (but not `let` or `const`) also become properties of the global `window` object.

```javascript
var globalVar = "I'm on the window!";
```

```
let globalLet = "I'm not directly on the window.";

console.log(window.globalVar); // *Output: I'm on the window!*
console.log(window.globalLet); // *Output: undefined*
```

The Danger of Global Scope: While easy access might seem convenient, having too many variables in the global scope is generally considered bad practice ("polluting the global scope"). Why?

- **Naming Collisions:** Different scripts or parts of your application might accidentally use the same global variable name, overwriting each other's values and causing unexpected behavior.
- **Maintainability:** It becomes harder to track where a global variable is being used or modified, making debugging difficult.

Modern JavaScript practices (like using modules, which we'll see in Chapter 16) strongly encourage minimizing the use of the global scope.

Function Scope

Before the introduction of `let` and `const` in ES6, JavaScript primarily had **function scope**. This means that variables declared using the `var` keyword *inside* a function are only accessible within that function and any functions nested inside it. They cannot be accessed from outside the function.

```
function calculateTotal(price, quantity) {
  // 'total' and 'taxRate' are local to this function
  var total = price * quantity;
  var taxRate = 0.08;
  var totalWithTax = total + (total * taxRate);

  console.log(`Total with tax: ${totalWithTax}`);

  function logCalculation() { // *Nested function*
      console.log(`Calculated ${total} before tax.`); // *Can access 'total'*
  }
  logCalculation();

  return totalWithTax;
}

let finalPrice = calculateTotal(50, 2);
console.log(`Final Price: ${finalPrice}`);
```

```
// *These would cause errors:*
// console.log(total); // ReferenceError: total is not defined
// console.log(taxRate); // ReferenceError: taxRate is not defined
```

Each function creates its own "bubble" of scope. This encapsulation is a good thing – it keeps the internal workings of a function contained and prevents interference with the outside world.

Block Scope

ES6 introduced `let` and `const`, and with them came **block scope**. A block is any section of code enclosed in curly braces {}. This includes `if` statements, `for` loops, `while` loops, and even standalone blocks.

Variables declared with `let` or `const` are scoped to the **nearest enclosing block**. They are only accessible *within* that block and any nested blocks.

```
let message = "Outside block";

if (true) {
  // 'blockVarLet' and 'blockVarConst' are block-scoped
  let blockVarLet = "Inside block (let)";
  const blockVarConst = "Inside block (const)";
  var blockVarVar = "Inside block (var)"; // 'var' ignores block scope!

  console.log(blockVarLet);    // *Accessible*
  console.log(blockVarConst);  // *Accessible*
  console.log(blockVarVar);    // *Accessible*
  console.log(message);        // *Accessible (from outer scope)*
}

console.log(message); // *Output: Outside block*

// *These cause errors because let/const are block-scoped:*
// console.log(blockVarLet); // ReferenceError: blockVarLet is not defined
// console.log(blockVarConst); // ReferenceError: blockVarConst is not defined

// *But 'var' declared inside the block IS accessible outside (function-scoped)!
*
console.log(blockVarVar); // *Output: Inside block (var)* - Often unexpected!
```

This difference is crucial, especially in loops:

```
// Using let (block-scoped) - Preferred
for (let i = 0; i < 3; i++) {
  console.log(`Inside loop (let): ${i}`);
}
// console.log(`Outside loop (let): ${i}`); // ReferenceError: i is not defined

// Using var (function-scoped) - Less Preferred
for (var j = 0; j < 3; j++) {
    console.log(`Inside loop (var): ${j}`);
}
console.log(`Outside loop (var): ${j}`); // *Output: 3 (j "leaked" outside the
loop)*
```

The block-scoping behavior of let and const is generally considered much more intuitive and helps prevent bugs caused by variables "leaking" out of blocks where they were intended to be temporary. This is a major reason why let and const are preferred over var in modern JavaScript.

Lexical Scoping (Scope Chains)

How does JavaScript find a variable when you use it? It uses **lexical scoping** (also called static scoping). This means that the accessibility of variables is determined by the *position* of the variables and blocks of scope *in the source code* when it's written, not by where the function is called from.

When your code tries to access a variable, JavaScript follows these steps:

1. It looks for the variable in the **current scope** (e.g., inside the currently executing function or block).
2. If it doesn't find the variable there, it looks in the **immediate outer scope** (the function or block that contains the current one).
3. If it's still not found, it continues searching outwards through successive outer scopes.
4. This continues until it reaches the **global scope**.
5. If the variable is not found even in the global scope, a ReferenceError usually occurs (unless you're assigning to it without let/const/var in non-strict mode, which creates an accidental global – another reason to avoid it!).

This sequence of nested scopes forms a **scope chain**.

```
let globalVar = "Global";
```

```
function outerFunction() {
  let outerVar = "Outer";

  function innerFunction() {
    let innerVar = "Inner";

    console.log(innerVar);   // *Found in innerFunction scope*
    console.log(outerVar);   // *Not in inner, found in outerFunction scope*
    console.log(globalVar);  // *Not in inner or outer, found in global scope*
  }

  innerFunction();
  // console.log(innerVar); // Error! Cannot access innerVar from outer scope
}

outerFunction();

// *Output:*
// Inner
// Outer
// Global
```

Lexical scoping ensures that a function "remembers" the environment (the scope chain) in which it was created, regardless of where it's later executed. This principle is fundamental to understanding closures, a more advanced topic related to functions remembering their surrounding state.

Hoisting

Now, let's address that other confusing behavior: sometimes it seems like you can use a variable or function *before* its declaration appears in the code. This happens because of **hoisting**.

Before your JavaScript code is executed line by line, the JavaScript engine first makes a pass through the code to find all variable and function *declarations* and conceptually "hoists" them to the top of their containing scope (global, function, or block for let/const).

Important: Hoisting only moves the **declarations**, not the **initializations** or assignments.

Let's see how hoisting affects var, let/const, and functions differently.

var **Hoisting**

Declarations using var are hoisted to the top of their function scope (or global scope) and are automatically initialized with the value undefined.

```
console.log(myVar); // *Output: undefined (Declaration hoisted, initialized
undefined)*

var myVar = "Hello!";

console.log(myVar); // *Output: Hello! (Assignment happens here)*

// What JavaScript conceptually does:
/*
var myVar; // Declaration hoisted and initialized undefined
console.log(myVar);
myVar = "Hello!"; // Assignment stays in place
console.log(myVar);
*/
```

Accessing myVar before the assignment doesn't cause an error, but it yields undefined, which can sometimes hide bugs.

let **and** const **Hoisting**

Declarations using let and const are **also hoisted** to the top of their *block* scope. However, unlike var, they are **not** initialized with any value (undefined or otherwise).

There's a period between the start of the block and the actual line where the let or const variable is declared. During this period, the variable is in the **Temporal Dead Zone (TDZ)**. Attempting to access the variable within the TDZ results in a ReferenceError.

```
// console.log(myLet); // ReferenceError: Cannot access 'myLet' before
initialization

let myLet = "I'm initialized now."; // TDZ ends here for myLet

console.log(myLet); // *Output: I'm initialized now.*

if (true) {
  // TDZ for blockConst starts here
  // console.log(blockConst); // ReferenceError! Still in TDZ
```

```
  const blockConst = "Initialized in block"; // TDZ ends here for blockConst
  console.log(blockConst); // *Output: Initialized in block*
}
```

The TDZ is actually a good thing! It prevents you from accidentally using a variable before its intended declaration and initialization, making code more robust and easier to reason about. It enforces discipline: declare before use.

Function Hoisting

How functions are hoisted depends on how they are defined:

1. **Function Declarations:** These are fully hoisted. Both the function name *and* its implementation are moved to the top of their scope. This means you can call a function declared this way *before* its definition appears in the code.

   ```
   declaredFunction(); // *Works! Output: I was declared!*

   function declaredFunction() {
     console.log("I was declared!");
   }

   // Conceptually:
   /*
   function declaredFunction() { // Declaration AND definition hoisted
     console.log("I was declared!");
   }
   declaredFunction();
   */
   ```

2. **Function Expressions:** Only the *variable declaration* part is hoisted (following the rules of var, let, or const). The actual function assignment remains where it is. Therefore, you **cannot** call a function expression before the line where it is assigned.

   ```
   // expressionVar(); // TypeError: expressionVar is not a function (if
   declared with var)
                     // ReferenceError: Cannot access 'expressionLet'
   before initialization (if let)

   var expressionVar = function() {
     console.log("I'm an expression (var)!");
   };
   ```

```
const expressionConst = function() {
  console.log("I'm an expression (const)!");
};

expressionVar();   // *Works now*
expressionConst(); // *Works now*
```

This difference is a key reason why the placement of function definitions matters, especially when using function expressions.

Practical Implications & Best Practices

Understanding scope and hoisting helps you write better code and debug issues more effectively.

- **Avoid Global Variables**: Minimize global scope pollution. Use modules or wrap code in functions to create local scopes.
- **Prefer let and const over var**: Block scope and the TDZ lead to more predictable and less error-prone code. Use const by default for variables that won't be reassigned.
- **Declare Before Use**: Even though hoisting exists, always declare your variables (let, const, var) and functions at the top of their relevant scope (block or function) before you use them. This makes code clearer and avoids TDZ errors.
- **Understand Function Hoisting Differences**: Be aware that function declarations can be called before definition, while function expressions cannot. Choose the definition style that fits your needs and maintain consistency.

Chapter Summary

In this chapter, we demystified **Scope** and **Hoisting**. We learned that scope dictates variable and function visibility, differentiating between **global scope, function scope** (primarily for var), and **block scope** (introduced by let and const). We explored **lexical scoping** and the **scope chain**, which determine how JavaScript looks up variables by searching outwards from the current scope. We then tackled **hoisting**, JavaScript's behavior of conceptually moving declarations to the top of their scope. We saw how var declarations are hoisted and initialized to undefined, while let and const are hoisted but remain uninitialized in the **Temporal Dead Zone (TDZ)** until their declaration line, causing a `ReferenceError` if accessed too early. We also contrasted the full hoisting of **function declarations** with the partial hoisting (variable declaration only) of **function expressions**. Finally, we established best practices like favoring `let/const`, avoiding globals, and declaring before use.

With a solid grasp of how JavaScript manages variable visibility and declarations, you're now equipped to write more complex and reliable code. The next logical step is to apply this knowledge to interact with the environment where JavaScript most commonly runs: the web browser. In Chapter 10, we'll dive into the **Document Object Model (DOM)**, learning how JavaScript can dynamically access and manipulate the content, structure, and style of web pages.

10
The DOM

Up until now, our JavaScript journey has focused on the core mechanics of the language itself – storing data in variables, performing operations, making decisions with conditionals, and repeating tasks with loops. We've built a solid foundation. But JavaScript truly comes alive when it starts interacting with its most common environment: the web browser. How does JavaScript change what you see on a webpage, react to your clicks, or update content dynamically? The answer lies in the **Document Object Model**, or **DOM**. This chapter is your gateway into understanding how JavaScript connects to and manipulates HTML documents, turning static pages into interactive experiences.

What is the DOM?

Imagine you've built a house using blueprints (your HTML code). The HTML defines the structure: walls, doors, windows, rooms. Now, you want to interact with that finished house – maybe paint a wall, open a window, or add a new piece of furniture. You need a way to represent the house's structure *programmatically* so you can target specific parts.

The **Document Object Model (DOM)** is precisely that representation for web pages. When a web browser loads an HTML document, it doesn't just display it; it creates a logical, tree-like structure in memory that represents all the elements, attributes, and text content of that page. This structure is the DOM. It's an **Application Program-**

ming Interface (API) – a set of rules and objects – that allows programming languages like JavaScript to access and manipulate the content, structure, and style of the HTML document.

Think of the DOM as a **live tree**:

- The document itself is the root of the tree.
- Every HTML tag (like <html>, <body>, <h1>, <p>, <div>) becomes a **node** (specifically, an *element node*) in the tree, branching off from its parent.
- The text content inside elements also becomes nodes (*text nodes*).
- Attributes of elements (like id, class, src, href) are also represented, often as properties of the element nodes.

JavaScript doesn't directly modify the raw HTML file. Instead, it interacts with this DOM tree structure in the browser's memory. Any changes JavaScript makes to the DOM tree are then instantly reflected in what the user sees on the rendered page.

```
<!-- Simple HTML -->
<!DOCTYPE html>
<html>
<head>
    <title>My Page</title>
</head>
<body>
    <h1>Welcome!</h1>
    <p id="intro">This is a paragraph.</p>
    <ul>
        <li>Item 1</li>
        <li>Item 2</li>
    </ul>
</body>
</html>
```

The browser would parse this HTML and create a DOM tree something like this (simplified):

```
Document
└─ html
    ├─ head
    │   ├─ #text ("\n    ")
    │   ├─ title
    │   │   └─ #text ("My Page")
    │   └─ #text ("\n")
    └─ body
```

```
├── #text ("\n    ")
├── h1
│   └── #text ("Welcome!")
├── #text ("\n    ")
├── p (id="intro")
│   └── #text ("This is a paragraph.")
├── #text ("\n    ")
├── ul
│   ├── #text ("\n        ")
│   ├── li
│   │   └── #text ("Item 1")
│   ├── #text ("\n        ")
│   ├── li
│   │   └── #text ("Item 2")
│   └── #text ("\n    ")
└── #text ("\n")
```

JavaScript gets access to this tree and can navigate it, select specific nodes (like the paragraph with id="intro"), and modify them.

The Document Object

The entry point for interacting with the DOM is the global document object, which is automatically provided by the browser environment. This object represents the entire HTML document loaded in the browser window or tab. It contains numerous properties and methods for accessing and manipulating the page.

You can explore this object directly in your browser's developer console (Chapter 1). Try typing document and pressing Enter. You'll see a representation of the current page's DOM structure.

All our interactions with the DOM will typically start with the document object.

Selecting Page Elements

Before you can change an element, style it, or read its content, you first need to *select* it – get a reference to that specific node in the DOM tree. JavaScript provides several methods attached to the document object (and sometimes other element nodes) for this purpose.

Let's use this sample HTML for our examples:

```
<!DOCTYPE html>
<html lang="en">
<head>
    <title>DOM Selection</title>
</head>
<body>
    <h1 id="main-heading">Learning DOM Selection</h1>
    <p class="content intro">This is the introduction paragraph.</p>
    <p class="content">This is another paragraph.</p>
    <div>
        <p>Paragraph inside a div.</p>
    </div>
    <ul id="item-list">
        <li class="item">Apple</li>
        <li class="item important">Banana</li>
        <li class="item">Cherry</li>
    </ul>

    <script src="app.js"></script>
</body>
</html>
```

Now, in our app.js file:

getElementById(id)

This is a classic and very efficient method if the element you want has a unique id attribute. It returns a **single element node** corresponding to that ID, or null if no element with that ID is found. Remember, IDs *should* be unique within a page.

```
// Select the h1 element using its ID
const headingElement = document.getElementById('main-heading');

// Select the ul element
const listElement = document.getElementById('item-list');

console.log(headingElement); // *Outputs the <h1> element object*
console.log(listElement);    // *Outputs the <ul> element object*

// Try selecting a non-existent ID
const missingElement = document.getElementById('non-existent');
console.log(missingElement); // *Output: null*
```

getElementsByTagName(tagName)

This method selects all elements with the specified HTML tag name (e.g., 'p', 'li', 'div'). It returns a **live HTMLCollection** of the found elements. An HTMLCollection is an array-like object (but not a true array). "Live" means that if elements with that tag name are added or removed from the DOM *after* you've selected the collection, the collection will automatically update.

```
// Select all paragraph elements
const allParagraphs = document.getElementsByTagName('p');
console.log(allParagraphs); // *Outputs an HTMLCollection of all <p> elements*
console.log(allParagraphs.length); // *Output: 3 (in our example)*

// Access a specific paragraph (remember, it's array-like, zero-indexed)
console.log(allParagraphs[0]); // *Outputs the first <p> element*
console.log(allParagraphs[1].textContent); // *Output: This is another
paragraph.*
```

getElementsByClassName(className)

Similar to getElementsByTagName, this selects all elements that have the specified CSS class name. It also returns a **live HTMLCollection**.

```
// Select all elements with the class 'item'
const listItems = document.getElementsByClassName('item');
console.log(listItems); // *Outputs an HTMLCollection of the <li> elements*
console.log(listItems.length); // *Output: 3*

// Select elements with the class 'content'
const contentParas = document.getElementsByClassName('content');
console.log(contentParas); // *Outputs an HTMLCollection [p.content.intro,
p.content]*
console.log(contentParas.length); // *Output: 2*
```

querySelector(cssSelector)

This is a very powerful and versatile modern method. It accepts a CSS selector string (the same kind you use in your CSS files!) and returns the **first element** in the document that matches the selector. If no match is found, it returns null. This is often preferred because you can use any valid CSS selector, making complex selections easier.

```javascript
// Select the first paragraph (matches the 'p' tag selector)
const firstPara = document.querySelector('p');
console.log(firstPara); // *Outputs the first <p> element*

// Select the element with ID 'main-heading' (using ID selector #)
const headingAgain = document.querySelector('#main-heading');
console.log(headingAgain); // *Outputs the <h1> element*

// Select the first element with class 'item' (using class selector .)
const firstItem = document.querySelector('.item');
console.log(firstItem); // *Outputs the first <li> element*

// Select the first element with class 'important' inside the element with ID
'item-list'
const importantItem = document.querySelector('#item-list .important');
console.log(importantItem); // *Outputs the <li> with class 'important'*

// Select a paragraph inside a div
const paraInDiv = document.querySelector('div p');
console.log(paraInDiv); // *Outputs the <p> inside the <div>*

// Select an element that doesn't exist
const nonExistent = document.querySelector('.missing');
console.log(nonExistent); // *Output: null*
```

querySelectorAll(cssSelector)

Similar to querySelector, but it returns **all** elements in the document that match the
provided CSS selector. It returns a **static NodeList**. A NodeList is also array-like, but
it's generally "static," meaning it won't automatically update if the DOM changes after
selection (unlike a live HTMLCollection). NodeLists also have some useful built-in
methods like forEach (which HTMLCollections often lack, though this is changing in
modern browsers).

```javascript
// Select all paragraph elements
const allParasAgain = document.querySelectorAll('p');
console.log(allParasAgain); // *Outputs a NodeList of all <p> elements*
console.log(allParasAgain.length); // *Output: 3*

// Select all elements with class 'item'
const allItems = document.querySelectorAll('.item');
console.log(allItems); // *Outputs a NodeList of the <li> elements*

// You can iterate over a NodeList easily using forEach
```

```
allItems.forEach(function(item, index) {
  console.log(`Item ${index}: ${item.textContent}`);
});
/* Output:
Item 0: Apple
Item 1: Banana
Item 2: Cherry
*/
```

Recommendation: For most modern development, `querySelector` (for single elements) and `querySelectorAll` (for multiple elements) are often the most convenient and powerful choices due to their ability to use any CSS selector. Use `getElementById` when you specifically need the performance benefit of selecting by a unique ID.

Manipulating Elements

Once you've selected an element node and have it stored in a variable, you can start manipulating it!

Changing Content

There are two primary properties for changing the content *inside* an element:

- `textContent`: Gets or sets the *text content* of an element and all its descendants, ignoring any HTML tags. It treats the content purely as text. This is generally **safer** and often faster when you only need to work with plain text.

  ```
  const introPara = document.querySelector('.intro');
  console.log(introPara.textContent); // *Output: This is the introduction
  paragraph.*

  // Change the text content
  introPara.textContent = "Welcome to the DOM manipulation section!";
  console.log(introPara.textContent); // *Output: Welcome to the DOM
  manipulation section!*

  // If you set textContent with HTML tags, they are treated as literal
  text
  introPara.textContent = "This text is <strong>important</strong>.";
  // *The paragraph will literally display "This text is
  <strong>important</strong>."*
  ```

- `innerHTML`: Gets or sets the *HTML content* (markup) within an element. The browser parses the string you provide as HTML. This is necessary if you need to insert or modify HTML structure within an element.

```
const list = document.getElementById('item-list');
console.log(list.innerHTML);
/* Output (roughly):
   <li class="item">Apple</li>
   <li class="item important">Banana</li>
   <li class="item">Cherry</li>
*/

// Change the HTML content
list.innerHTML = '<li class="new">First new item</li><li
class="new">Second new item</li>';
console.log(list.innerHTML);
/* Output:
   <li class="new">First new item</li><li class="new">Second new
item</li>
*/
```

Security Warning: Be extremely careful when setting `innerHTML` using content that comes from user input or external sources. If the content contains malicious `<script>` tags or other harmful HTML, setting it via `innerHTML` can execute that script, leading to Cross-Site Scripting (XSS) vulnerabilities. **Always sanitize or escape external content before using it with** `innerHTML`. Prefer `textContent` whenever you are dealing only with text.

Changing Styles

You can directly manipulate the inline styles of an element using its `style` property. The `style` property itself is an object, where each property corresponds to a CSS property.

Important: CSS properties with hyphens (kebab-case) like `background-color` or `font-size` are converted to camelCase in JavaScript (e.g., `backgroundColor`, `font-Size`).

```
const heading = document.getElementById('main-heading');

// Change the color
heading.style.color = 'blue';
```

```
// Change the background color (kebab-case to camelCase)
heading.style.backgroundColor = 'lightgray';

// Change font size
heading.style.fontSize = '3em'; // *Value must be a string, including units*

// Add padding
heading.style.padding = '10px';

// Remove a style by setting it to an empty string
heading.style.padding = '';
```

While direct style manipulation works, it sets *inline styles* (<h1 style="...">), which can be harder to manage and override than using CSS classes. For more significant style changes or reusable styles, it's often better practice to define CSS classes in your stylesheet and then use JavaScript to **add or remove those classes** from the element using the classList property (e.g., element.classList.add('active'), element.-classList.remove('highlight')).

Modifying Attributes

You can read, set, and remove HTML attributes (like id, class, src, href, alt, etc.) using dedicated methods:

- getAttribute(attributeName): Returns the current value of the specified attribute as a string, or null if the attribute doesn't exist.
- setAttribute(attributeName, value): Adds a new attribute or changes the value of an existing attribute. The value is typically a string.
- removeAttribute(attributeName): Removes the specified attribute from the element.

```
const introPara = document.querySelector('.intro');

// Get the class attribute
let currentClasses = introPara.getAttribute('class');
console.log(currentClasses); // *Output: content intro*

// Set the 'data-status' attribute (custom data attribute)
introPara.setAttribute('data-status', 'updated');

// Add an ID attribute
introPara.setAttribute('id', 'introduction');
```

```
// Change the class attribute
introPara.setAttribute('class', 'content updated-intro');

console.log(introPara.getAttribute('data-status')); // *Output: updated*
console.log(introPara.getAttribute('id')); // *Output: introduction*

// Remove the data-status attribute
introPara.removeAttribute('data-status');
console.log(introPara.getAttribute('data-status')); // *Output: null*
```

Direct Property Access: For many common standard HTML attributes (id, class-Name, src, href, value, etc.), JavaScript also provides direct properties on the element node that you can access and modify more easily.

```
const heading = document.getElementById('main-heading');
const list = document.getElementById('item-list');

// Access ID directly
console.log(heading.id); // *Output: main-heading*

// Modify ID directly
heading.id = 'new-main-heading';
console.log(heading.id); // *Output: new-main-heading*

// Access class name(s) as a string
console.log(list.className); // *Output: (Might be empty if set via classList
initially)*

// Set class name(s) directly (overwrites existing classes)
list.className = 'items active';
console.log(list.className); // *Output: items active*
```

While convenient, direct property access might behave slightly differently than get-Attribute/setAttribute for certain attributes (especially boolean attributes or those involving URLs). Using getAttribute/setAttribute is sometimes more consistent, particularly for custom attributes. For managing classes, using element.classList is generally the recommended modern approach.

Creating and Adding Elements

The DOM isn't static; JavaScript can create entirely new HTML elements from scratch and insert them into the page structure.

The typical workflow is:

1. **Create** the new element node using `document.createElement(tagName)`.
2. **Configure** the new element (set its content, attributes, styles).
3. **Append** the new element to an existing element in the DOM tree.

```
// 1. Create a new list item element
const newListItem = document.createElement('li'); // *Creates an empty
<li></li>*

// 2. Configure the new element
newListItem.textContent = 'Durian'; // *Set its text content*
newListItem.setAttribute('class', 'item exotic'); // *Set its class*
// *Alternatively: newListItem.className = 'item exotic';*
// *Or better: newListItem.classList.add('item', 'exotic');*

// 3. Append the new element to the existing list
const itemList = document.getElementById('item-list');
itemList.appendChild(newListItem); // *Adds the new <li> to the end of the <ul>*

// Let's add another one
const anotherItem = document.createElement('li');
anotherItem.textContent = 'Mango';
anotherItem.classList.add('item'); // *Using classList is often cleaner*
itemList.appendChild(anotherItem);

console.log(itemList.innerHTML); // *Shows the updated list with Durian and
Mango*
```

- `appendChild(childNode)`: Adds the `childNode` as the *last* child of the parent element it's called on.

Other methods for adding nodes include:

- `insertBefore(newNode, referenceNode)`: Inserts `newNode` before `referenceNode` within the parent.
- Modern methods like `append()`, `prepend()`, `before()`, `after()` offer more flexibility for adding multiple nodes or text directly, but `appendChild` is the classic method.

Removing Elements

You can also remove elements from the DOM.

removeChild(childNode) (Classic)

The traditional way requires getting a reference to the **parent** element and then calling `removeChild()` on the parent, passing the child element you want to remove.

```
const list = document.getElementById('item-list');
const itemToRemove = document.querySelector('#item-list .important'); // *Select
Banana*

if (list && itemToRemove) {
  let removed = list.removeChild(itemToRemove);
  console.log("Removed element:", removed); // *Outputs the removed <li>
element*
}

console.log(list.innerHTML); // *Shows the list without Banana*
```

element.remove() (Modern)

A much simpler, modern way is to call the `remove()` method directly on the element you want to remove.

```
const itemToRemoveDirectly = document.querySelector('#item-list .exotic'); //
*Select Durian*

if (itemToRemoveDirectly) {
  itemToRemoveDirectly.remove(); // *Removes the Durian li directly*
}

console.log(list.innerHTML); // *Shows the list without Banana and Durian*
```

element.remove() is generally preferred for its simplicity when browser compatibility allows (it's widely supported in modern browsers).

Introduction to Events

We've seen how to select, modify, create, and delete elements, giving us full control over the structure and appearance of a page *after* it loads. But the real magic of dynamic web pages happens when they *react* to user actions – mouse clicks, key presses, form submissions, window resizing, etc.

The DOM provides a mechanism for this called **Events**. JavaScript can "listen" for specific events occurring on specific elements. When an event occurs (like a button being clicked), a predefined JavaScript function (an "event handler" or "event listener") can be executed automatically.

```
// --- Preview of Chapter 11 ---

// Get a button element (assuming <button id="myButton">Click Me</button>
exists)
// const myButton = document.getElementById('myButton');

// Add an event listener for the 'click' event
// myButton.addEventListener('click', function() {
//   alert('Button was clicked!');
//   // Or change some DOM element...
// });

// --- End Preview ---
```

This ability to attach behavior to user interactions is what bridges the gap between a static document and an interactive application.

Chapter Summary

This chapter introduced the **Document Object Model (DOM)**, the browser's representation of an HTML document as a programmable tree structure. We learned that the global `document` object is our entry point. We explored various methods for **selecting elements**: `getElementById`, `getElementsByTagName`, `getElementsByClassName`, and the versatile `querySelector` and `querySelectorAll` which use CSS selectors. We then covered manipulating selected elements: changing content with `textContent` (safer) and `innerHTML` (powerful but requires caution), modifying inline styles via the `style` property, and managing attributes with `getAttribute`, `setAttribute`, `removeAttribute`, alongside direct property access. We also learned how to dynamically **create** new elements (`createElement`), configure them, and **add** them to the DOM (`appendChild`), as well as how to **remove** elements (`removeChild`, `element.remove()`). Finally, we briefly introduced the concept of **Events**, setting the stage for making our pages truly interactive.

You now have the fundamental skills to read and change web pages using JavaScript. The next crucial step is learning how to respond to user actions. In Chapter 11, we will dive deeply into **Events**, exploring how to listen for clicks, key presses, mouse movements, and more, allowing you to build truly dynamic and responsive user interfaces.

11

Events in Depth

In the previous chapter, we learned how to use JavaScript to find and manipulate elements on a web page through the DOM. We can now change text, update styles, add new elements, and remove old ones. That's powerful, but it's only half the story of dynamic web pages. The real interactivity comes when our pages *react* to things that happen – a user clicking a button, typing in a field, moving the mouse, or even just resizing the browser window. These occurrences are known as **Events**. This chapter dives deep into how JavaScript handles events, allowing you to "listen" for specific actions and trigger code in response, making your web pages truly responsive and engaging.

The Event Listener

The standard and most flexible way to make an element react to an event is by attaching an **event listener**. You select the target element (using methods from Chapter 10) and then call its addEventListener() method.

The basic syntax is:

```
targetElement.addEventListener(eventType, listenerFunction);
```

Let's break this down:

- targetElement: The specific DOM element you want to listen to (e.g., a button, a paragraph, the entire document or window).
- addEventListener: The method you call on that element.
- eventType: A string specifying the name of the event you want to listen for (e.g., 'click', 'mouseover', 'keydown'). There are many different event types, which we'll explore shortly. **Note:** The 'on' prefix (like onclick) used in older HTML attributes or property assignments is *not* included here.
- listenerFunction: The function that will be executed **when the specified event occurs on the target element**. This function is often called an "event handler" or "callback function". You can provide a reference to a named function or define an anonymous function directly (as we saw with function expressions in Chapter 8).

Let's add a simple click listener to a button. Assume we have this HTML:

```
<!DOCTYPE html>
<html>
<head><title>Event Listener</title></head>
<body>
    <button id="myButton">Click Me!</button>
    <p id="messageArea"></p>

    <script src="app.js"></script>
</body>
</html>
```

And in app.js:

```
// 1. Select the elements
const button = document.getElementById('myButton');
const messageArea = document.getElementById('messageArea');

// 2. Define the listener function
function handleButtonClick() {
  messageArea.textContent = 'Button was clicked! Thanks!';
  console.log('Button click handled.');
}

// 3. Attach the listener
button.addEventListener('click', handleButtonClick);

// *You could also use an anonymous function directly:*
// button.addEventListener('click', function() {
//   messageArea.textContent = 'Button clicked via anonymous function!';
```

```
//    console.log('Anonymous click handler ran.');
// });
```

Now, every time you click the "Click Me!" button on the page, the `handleButtonClick` function will execute, updating the paragraph's text and logging a message to the console.

You can add multiple listeners for the same event type to a single element, and they will all execute when the event occurs.

A Note on Older Methods: You might encounter older ways of attaching event handlers, like setting `onclick` directly as an HTML attribute (`<button onclick="handle-ButtonClick()">`) or as a property in JavaScript (`button.onclick = handleButton-Click;`). While these sometimes work for simple cases, `addEventListener` is generally preferred because:

- It allows adding multiple listeners for the same event. Setting `element.on-click` multiple times just overwrites the previous handler.
- It provides more control over the event handling phases (bubbling vs. capturing, discussed later).
- It helps keep JavaScript logic separate from HTML structure.

Stick with `addEventListener` for modern development.

The Event Object

When an event occurs and your listener function is called, the browser automatically passes a special object as the first argument to your function. This is the **Event object**, and it contains valuable information about the event that just happened.

You need to include a parameter in your listener function definition to receive this object (conventionally named `event`, `evt`, or simply `e`).

```
function handleButtonClick(event) { // *Parameter 'event' receives the Event
object*
  console.log('Event object received:', event);

  // Access properties of the event object
  console.log('Type of event:', event.type); // *e.g., "click"*
  console.log('Element that triggered event:', event.target); // *The button
itself*
  console.log('Element listener is attached to:', event.currentTarget);
```

```
    messageArea.textContent = `Event type "${event.type}" occurred!`;
}

button.addEventListener('click', handleButtonClick);
```

Some essential properties and methods of the Event object include:

- `event.type`: A string indicating the type of event that fired (e.g., `"click"`, `"mouseover"`).
- `event.target`: A reference to the specific DOM element that **originated** the event. This is crucial for event delegation (discussed later). For example, if you click on text *inside* a button, `event.target` might be the text node, while `currentTarget` would still be the button the listener is attached to.
- `event.currentTarget`: A reference to the element the event listener is **currently attached to** as the event propagates through the DOM. In simple cases without propagation concerns, it's often the same as `event.target`.
- `event.preventDefault()`: A method you can call to **stop** the browser's default action associated with that event (if any). For example, stopping a link from navigating or a form from submitting.
- `event.stopPropagation()`: A method to **stop** the event from propagating further through the DOM (typically stops the "bubbling" phase, which we'll cover soon).
- **Coordinates (Mouse Events):** Properties like `event.clientX`, `event.clientY` provide the mouse pointer's coordinates relative to the browser window's visible area when the event occurred. `event.pageX`, `event.pageY` provide coordinates relative to the entire document.
- **Key Information (Keyboard Events):** Properties like `event.key` (e.g., `"a"`, `"Enter"`, `"Shift"`) and `event.code` (e.g., `"KeyA"`, `"Enter"`, `"ShiftLeft"`) provide details about the key that was pressed.

Exploring the event object in the console (`console.log(event)`) is a great way to discover the specific information available for different event types.

Common Event Types

There's a wide variety of events you can listen for. Here are some common categories and examples:

Mouse Events

These relate to interactions with the mouse pointer.

- click: Fired when the primary mouse button is clicked (pressed and released) on an element.
- dblclick: Fired when the primary mouse button is double-clicked on an element.
- mousedown: Fired when the mouse button is pressed *down* over an element.
- mouseup: Fired when the mouse button is released over an element.
- mouseover: Fired when the mouse pointer moves *onto* an element or one of its children.
- mouseout: Fired when the mouse pointer moves *off* of an element or one of its children.
- mousemove: Fired repeatedly as the mouse pointer moves while it is over an element. (Use with caution, as it can fire very frequently!).

```
const box = document.getElementById('hoverBox'); // *Assume <div
id="hoverBox"></div>*

box.addEventListener('mouseover', function(e) {
  e.target.style.backgroundColor = 'lightblue';
  console.log('Mouse entered the box!');
});

box.addEventListener('mouseout', function(e) {
  e.target.style.backgroundColor = 'lightgray'; // *Reset background*
  console.log('Mouse left the box!');
});
```

Keyboard Events

These relate to keyboard input. They are often listened for on the document or specific input fields.

- keydown: Fired when a key is pressed *down*. Fires repeatedly if the key is held down. Good for detecting actions like Enter or Shift.
- keyup: Fired when a key is *released*.
- keypress: (Legacy) Fired when a key that produces a character value (like 'a', '5', not Shift or F1) is pressed down. It's generally recommended to use keydown or keyup instead for better consistency across browsers and input methods.

```
const inputField = document.getElementById('myInput'); // *Assume <input
id="myInput">*

inputField.addEventListener('keydown', function(event) {
  console.log(`Key pressed: ${event.key} (Code: ${event.code})`);
  if (event.key === 'Enter') {
      console.log('Enter key was pressed in the input field!');
      // *Maybe submit a form or perform an action*
  }
});
```

Form Events

These relate to interactions with HTML forms and form elements.

- submit: Fired on the <form> element when the user attempts to submit it (e.g., by clicking a submit button or pressing Enter in a field). Often used with event.preventDefault() to perform validation before allowing submission.
- change: Fired for <input>, <select>, and <textarea> elements when their value is committed by the user (e.g., after selecting a dropdown option, checking/unchecking a checkbox, or when an input field loses focus after its value was changed).
- input: Fired **immediately** for <input> or <textarea> elements whenever their value changes. Useful for real-time feedback or filtering as the user types.
- focus: Fired when an element (like an input field) receives focus (e.g., the user clicks on it or tabs to it).
- blur: Fired when an element loses focus.

```
const myForm = document.getElementById('myForm'); // *Assume <form id="myForm">*

myForm.addEventListener('submit', function(event) {
  console.log('Form submission attempt detected.');
  // *Often, you'll prevent the default submission to handle it with JS:*
  event.preventDefault();
  console.log('Default form submission prevented.');
  // *Perform validation or send data via fetch (Chapter 17) here*
});

const emailInput = document.getElementById('email'); // *Assume <input
id="email">*
emailInput.addEventListener('input', function(e) {
    console.log(`Email field value changed to: ${e.target.value}`);
```

```
});
```

Window and Document Events

These relate to the browser window or the document loading process.

- `load`: Fired on the `window` object when the entire page, including all resources (images, stylesheets, etc.), has completely finished loading.
- `DOMContentLoaded`: Fired on the `document` object when the initial HTML document has been completely loaded and parsed, **without** waiting for stylesheets, images, and subframes to finish loading. This event often fires much earlier than `load` and is usually the preferred event for running JavaScript code that needs to interact with the DOM as soon as it's ready.
- `resize`: Fired on the `window` object when the browser window is resized.
- `scroll`: Fired on the `document` or specific scrollable elements when the user scrolls. (Like `mousemove`, can fire frequently).

```
// *Common pattern: Wait for DOM to be ready before running JS that needs it*
document.addEventListener('DOMContentLoaded', function() {
  console.log('DOM fully loaded and parsed!');
  // *It's now safe to select and manipulate elements*
  const mainHeading = document.getElementById('main-heading');
  if(mainHeading) {
      mainHeading.style.color = 'purple';
  }
});

window.addEventListener('resize', function() {
    console.log(`Window resized to: ${window.innerWidth}x$
{window.innerHeight}`);
});
```

Event Propagation

What happens if you have nested elements, and both the inner element and an outer element have event listeners for the same event type (like 'click')? Which listener runs first? This is governed by **event propagation**.

Events travel through the DOM in two main phases:

1. **Capturing Phase:** The event travels *down* the DOM tree from the `window` to the `document`, down to the parent elements, and finally reaches the `event.target` (the element where the event originated). Listeners attached for the capturing phase run during this journey downwards.

2. **Bubbling Phase:** After reaching the target, the event travels back *up* the DOM tree from the `event.target` through its ancestors, back up to the `document` and `window`. Listeners attached for the bubbling phase run during this journey upwards.

By default, `addEventListener` **attaches listeners for the bubbling phase.** This is the most common and often most intuitive model.

Imagine this HTML:

```
<div id="outerDiv" style="padding: 30px; background-color: lightblue;">
  Outer Div
  <button id="innerButton" style="padding: 10px; background-color: lightcoral;">
    Inner Button
  </button>
</div>
```

And this JavaScript:

```
const outerDiv = document.getElementById('outerDiv');
const innerButton = document.getElementById('innerButton');

outerDiv.addEventListener('click', function(event) {
  console.log('Outer Div Clicked! Target:', event.target.id);
});

innerButton.addEventListener('click', function(event) {
  console.log('Inner Button Clicked! Target:', event.target.id);
});
```

If you click the **Inner Button**:

1. The click event originates on the button (`event.target` is `innerButton`).
2. The button's click listener runs: "Inner Button Clicked! Target: innerButton".
3. The event **bubbles up** to the `outerDiv`.
4. The `outerDiv`'s click listener runs: "Outer Div Clicked! Target: innerButton" (notice `event.target` is still the button where the click originated).

Stopping Propagation: Sometimes, you want to handle an event on an inner element and prevent it from triggering listeners on ancestor elements. You can do this by calling `event.stopPropagation()` inside the inner element's listener.

```
innerButton.addEventListener('click', function(event) {
  console.log('Inner Button Clicked (propagation stopped)!');
  event.stopPropagation(); // *Stop the event from bubbling up*
});

// *Now, if you click the inner button, only the button's listener runs.*
// *The outer div's listener will NOT run for clicks on the button.*
```

Capturing Phase (Less Common): You can explicitly attach a listener to the capturing phase by passing `true` or `{ capture: true }` as the third argument to `addEventListener`. Capturing listeners run *before* bubbling listeners. This is less frequently needed but can be useful in specific scenarios like intercepting events early.

```
// *Listener attached to run during the capture phase*
// outerDiv.addEventListener('click', function(event) {
//   console.log('Outer Div Clicked (Capture Phase)');
// }, true);
```

Preventing Default Browser Actions

As mentioned, certain HTML elements have built-in browser behaviors associated with specific events.

- Clicking a link (`<a>` tag with an `href`) navigates to that URL.
- Clicking a submit button inside a `<form>` submits the form data and usually reloads the page.
- Pressing certain keys in input fields might trigger default actions.

Often, you want to intercept these actions and handle them with your own JavaScript logic. The `event.preventDefault()` method is used for this.

Example: Form Validation

```
<form id="signupForm">
  <label for="email">Email:</label>
  <input type="email" id="email" required>
  <p id="emailError" style="color: red; display: none;">Please enter a valid
email.</p>
```

```
    <button type="submit">Sign Up</button>
</form>

const signupForm = document.getElementById('signupForm');
const emailInput = document.getElementById('email');
const emailError = document.getElementById('emailError');

signupForm.addEventListener('submit', function(event) {
  console.log('Submit event fired.');

  // *Simple validation: check if email contains '@'*
  if (!emailInput.value.includes('@')) {
    console.log('Validation failed. Preventing submission.');
    emailError.style.display = 'block'; // *Show error message*
    event.preventDefault(); // *STOP the form from actually submitting*
  } else {
    console.log('Validation passed. Allowing submission (or handling via JS).');
    emailError.style.display = 'none'; // *Hide error message*
    // *If you wanted to submit via JavaScript (e.g., using fetch):*
    // event.preventDefault(); // *Still prevent default*
    // *... your fetch code here ...*
  }
});
```

By calling `event.preventDefault()` when validation fails, we stop the browser's default form submission process, allowing us to display an error message instead.

Event Delegation

Consider a long list (`<ul>`) where each list item (`<li>`) needs to react to a click. Attaching an individual event listener to *every single* `<li>` can become inefficient, especially if the list is very long or items are frequently added and removed dynamically.

Event delegation provides a more efficient solution by leveraging event bubbling. Instead of attaching listeners to each child element, you attach a **single listener** to a common ancestor element (like the parent `<ul>`).

Inside the parent's listener, you use `event.target` to determine which specific child element actually triggered the event.

```
<ul id="parent-list">
  <li data-id="item-1">Item 1</li>
  <li data-id="item-2">Item 2</li>
  <li data-id="item-3">Item 3</li>
```

```
  <!-- Many more items... -->
</ul>
<p id="delegationMessage"></p>

const parentList = document.getElementById('parent-list');
const delegationMsg = document.getElementById('delegationMessage');

// Attach ONE listener to the parent UL
parentList.addEventListener('click', function(event) {
  console.log(`Click detected inside UL. Target:`, event.target);

  // *Check if the clicked element (event.target) is actually an LI*
  if (event.target.tagName === 'LI') {
    // *Or check if it has a specific class: if
(event.target.classList.contains('item'))*

    // *Access data from the clicked LI*
    const itemId = event.target.getAttribute('data-id') ||
event.target.textContent;

    delegationMsg.textContent = `You clicked on list item: ${itemId}`;

    // *Optionally, stop propagation if needed*
    // event.stopPropagation();
  } else {
      delegationMsg.textContent = `You clicked inside the UL, but not on an
item.`;
  }
});

// *If you later add more LIs dynamically using JS, this listener*
// *will automatically work for them too!*
// const newItem = document.createElement('li');
// newItem.textContent = 'Item 4 (added later)';
// parentList.appendChild(newItem);
```

Benefits of Event Delegation:

- **Performance**: Fewer event listeners attached means less memory usage and setup time.
- **Simplicity**: Easier to manage one listener than potentially hundreds.
- **Dynamic Elements**: Automatically works for elements added to the parent *after* the listener was attached, without needing to add new listeners explicitly.

Event delegation is a powerful and common pattern in JavaScript event handling.

Chapter Summary

This chapter illuminated the world of **Events** in JavaScript, the key to creating interactive web experiences. We learned how to attach **event listeners** using `addEventListener(eventType, listenerFunction)` to make elements react to occurrences. We explored the crucial **Event object**, passed automatically to listener functions, which provides vital details about the event (`event.type`, `event.target`). We surveyed **common event types** across categories like mouse, keyboard, form, and window events. The concept of **event propagation** (bubbling and capturing) was explained, showing how events travel through the DOM and how `event.stopPropagation()` can halt this process. We learned how to use `event.preventDefault()` to override default browser behaviors for elements like links and forms. Finally, we uncovered the efficient **event delegation** pattern, where a single listener on a parent element can handle events for many child elements by inspecting `event.target`.

You can now make your web pages respond to user actions, bridging the gap between static documents and dynamic applications. However, many web interactions aren't instantaneous. Actions like fetching data from a server, waiting for user input over time, or setting timers involve delays. JavaScript needs a way to handle these time-delayed operations without freezing the browser. In the next chapter, we'll begin exploring **Asynchronous JavaScript**, starting with the traditional approach using callback functions.

12
Asynchronous JavaScript and Callbacks

In the last couple of chapters, we learned how to bring web pages to life. We can select elements with the DOM (Chapter 10) and make them react to user interactions using events (Chapter 11). Clicking a button can now trigger a function that changes text or styles – it all feels instantaneous. However, many common web operations *aren't* instantaneous.

Think about these scenarios:

- Fetching user data from a remote server across the internet.
- Waiting for a user to upload a large file.
- Setting a timer to execute a piece of code after a few seconds.
- Reading data from the computer's local storage.

These tasks take time, ranging from milliseconds to potentially many seconds or even minutes. How does JavaScript, which we've seen execute line by line, handle these delays without making the entire browser freeze? This chapter introduces the fundamental concept of **asynchronous programming** in JavaScript and explores the traditional mechanism used to manage it: **callback functions**.

Synchronous vs. Asynchronous Code

To understand asynchronous operations, let's first clarify what **synchronous** means. Most of the code we've written so far has been synchronous.

- **Synchronous Execution:** Code executes line by line, one statement at a time. Each statement must complete before the next one can begin. If a statement takes a long time to finish, the entire program waits.

  Think of it like a single-lane road – one car must pass a point before the next one can. Or imagine making a phone call – you wait for the other person to answer and complete the conversation before you can do something else.

  ```
  console.log("First Task: Starting");
  // *Imagine a time-consuming synchronous task here*
  // *e.g., a complex calculation (though hard to simulate well)*
  // *for (let i = 0; i < 1_000_000_000; i++) { /* busy work */ }*
  console.log("Second Task: Finished the (blocking) first task.");
  console.log("Third Task: All done.");
  ```

  In truly synchronous code, "Second Task" wouldn't print until the time-consuming task was completely finished.

- **Asynchronous Execution:** Allows the program to initiate a task that might take time (like fetching data) and then *move on* to the next line of code *without waiting* for the initiated task to complete. When the long-running task eventually finishes, a mechanism (like a callback function) is used to handle its result or notify the program.

  Think of ordering food at a counter where they give you a buzzer. You place your order (initiate the task), then you can go sit down or chat with friends (move on to other tasks). When the food is ready (task completes), the buzzer rings (notification), and you go collect your food (handle the result). The key is that you weren't stuck waiting at the counter the whole time.

  ```
  console.log("First Task: Ordering food (starting async task)");

  // *setTimeout simulates an async operation that takes time*
  setTimeout(function() {
      // *This function (the callback) runs LATER*
      console.log("Async Task Complete: Food is ready!");
  }, 2000); // *2000 milliseconds = 2 seconds delay*
  ```

```
console.log("Second Task: Got my buzzer, doing other things...");
console.log("Third Task: Still waiting for food, but not blocked.");

// *Output Order:*
// First Task: Ordering food (starting async task)
// Second Task: Got my buzzer, doing other things...
// Third Task: Still waiting for food, but not blocked.
// (after ~2 seconds)
// Async Task Complete: Food is ready!
```

Notice how the second and third tasks print *before* the asynchronous task completes. The program didn't wait.

The Problem with Blocking Code

Why is this distinction so important, especially in web browsers? JavaScript in the browser (for the most part related to user interface updates) runs in a **single thread**. Think of this thread as a single worker responsible for handling everything: running your JavaScript code, updating what the user sees on the screen (rendering HTML and CSS), and responding to user interactions (like clicks and scrolling).

If you execute a long-running **synchronous** task on this single thread, the worker gets completely occupied with that task. While it's busy, it **cannot** do anything else. This leads to:

- **Frozen User Interface (UI):** The page becomes unresponsive. Buttons won't react to clicks, animations stop, scrolling halts.
- **Poor User Experience:** Users see a stuck page and might think the website or even their browser has crashed.
- **"Browser Unresponsive" Warnings:** The browser itself might detect that the page is stuck and prompt the user to wait or close the page.

Consider the built-in `alert()` function. While simple, it's actually a *synchronous*, blocking function.

```
console.log("Before alert");
alert("This blocks everything! Click OK to continue."); // *UI freezes here*
console.log("After alert"); // *This only runs after OK is clicked*
```

While `alert` is an obvious example, any synchronous JavaScript operation that takes significant time (complex calculations, processing large amounts of data synchronously) can cause the same blocking problem.

Therefore, operations that inherently involve waiting (like network requests, timers, file I/O) **must** be handled asynchronously in JavaScript to keep the main thread free and the user interface responsive.

Asynchronous Operations in Action

Let's revisit `setTimeout`, a built-in browser function that perfectly illustrates the asynchronous pattern.

Syntax: `setTimeout(callbackFunction, delayInMilliseconds)`

- `callbackFunction`: The function to be executed *after* the delay.
- `delayInMilliseconds`: The minimum time (in milliseconds) to wait before executing the callback. 1000ms = 1 second.

```
console.log("Program Start");

setTimeout(function reportLater() {
  // *This is the callback function*
  console.log("Timer finished after 1.5 seconds!");
}, 1500); // *Wait 1.5 seconds*

console.log("setTimeout requested, but program continues...");

setTimeout(function reportSooner() {
  console.log("Timer finished after 0.5 seconds!");
}, 500); // *Wait 0.5 seconds*

console.log("Program End");

// *Expected Output Order:*
// Program Start
// setTimeout requested, but program continues...
// Program End
// (after ~0.5 seconds)
// Timer finished after 0.5 seconds!
// (after ~1.5 seconds from start)
// Timer finished after 1.5 seconds!
```

Key takeaways from `setTimeout`:

1. Calling `setTimeout` does **not** pause the program's execution. It simply schedules the `callbackFunction` to be run later.
2. The code following the `setTimeout` call executes immediately.
3. The callback functions execute only after their respective delays have passed *and* the main JavaScript thread is free.

How does this work behind the scenes? (Simplified View) Browsers manage asynchronous operations using an **event loop** and a **callback queue**.

- When you call `setTimeout`, the browser's timer mechanism takes note of the callback and the delay.
- Your main JavaScript code continues running.
- When the timer finishes, the browser places the `callbackFunction` into the callback queue.
- The **event loop** continuously checks if the main JavaScript execution stack is empty.
- If the stack is empty *and* there's a function waiting in the callback queue, the event loop takes the function from the queue and pushes it onto the execution stack, running it.

This mechanism ensures that asynchronous callbacks don't interrupt currently running synchronous code and only execute when the main thread is available, keeping the UI responsive. You don't need to manage the event loop directly, but understanding its existence helps clarify why async code behaves the way it does.

Callback Functions

We saw `setTimeout` uses a function passed as an argument (a callback) to execute code later. This pattern – passing a function to be called upon completion – is the core idea behind traditional asynchronous handling in JavaScript.

Let's simulate a function that "fetches" user data asynchronously.

```
function fetchUserData(userId, callback) {
  console.log(`Fetching data for user ${userId}...`);

  // *Simulate network delay*
  setTimeout(function() {
    // *Simulate finding the data*
    const userData = {
        id: userId,
        name: `User ${userId}`,
```

```
      email: `user${userId}@example.com`
    };
    console.log(`Data found for user ${userId}.`);

    // *Execute the callback function, passing the data back*
    callback(userData);
  }, 1000); // *Simulate 1 second delay*
}

// *Define the function to handle the data once it arrives*
function displayUserData(user) {
  console.log("--- User Data Received ---");
  console.log(`Name: ${user.name}`);
  console.log(`Email: ${user.email}`);
  console.log("------------------------");
}

// *Call fetchUserData, providing displayUserData as the callback*
console.log("Requesting user data...");
fetchUserData(123, displayUserData);
console.log("Request sent, waiting for data...");

// *Output:*
// Requesting user data...
// Fetching data for user 123...
// Request sent, waiting for data...
// (after ~1 second)
// Data found for user 123.
// --- User Data Received ---
// Name: User 123
// Email: user123@example.com
// ------------------------
```

In this example:

1. We call `fetchUserData`, passing the user ID and the `displayUserData` function.
2. `fetchUserData` starts the simulated delay using `setTimeout`.
3. Our main code continues and prints "Request sent...".
4. After the delay, the `setTimeout` callback runs inside `fetchUserData`.
5. It creates the `userData` object.
6. Crucially, it then calls the `callback` function we originally provided (`displayUserData`), passing the `userData` object as an argument.
7. `displayUserData` executes, logging the received information.

The callback function acts as a bridge, allowing the asynchronous operation (`fetch-UserData`) to deliver its result back to the part of the code that needs it, once the result is ready.

Callback Hell

Callbacks work well for simple asynchronous operations. However, problems arise when you need to perform **multiple asynchronous operations in sequence**, where each step depends on the result of the previous one.

Imagine needing to:

1. Get a user ID.
2. Use the ID to fetch user details.
3. Use the user details to fetch their recent posts.

Using the callback pattern, each step would involve nesting the next asynchronous call inside the callback of the previous one:

```
function step1(callback) {
  console.log("Step 1: Getting User ID...");
  setTimeout(() => {
    const userId = 5; // *Simulated result*
    console.log("Step 1 Complete. User ID:", userId);
    callback(userId); // *Pass result to next step's function*
  }, 500);
}

function step2(userId, callback) {
  console.log("Step 2: Fetching Details for User", userId);
  setTimeout(() => {
    const userDetails = { name: "Alice", id: userId }; // *Simulated result*
    console.log("Step 2 Complete. Details:", userDetails);
    callback(userDetails); // *Pass result to next step's function*
  }, 500);
}

function step3(userDetails, callback) {
  console.log("Step 3: Fetching Posts for User", userDetails.name);
  setTimeout(() => {
    const posts = ["Post A", "Post B"]; // *Simulated result*
    console.log("Step 3 Complete. Posts:", posts);
    callback(posts); // *Pass result to final handler*
  }, 500);
}
```

```
// --- The Nested Structure ---
console.log("Starting sequential async operations...");

step1(function(receivedUserId) { // *Callback for step 1*
  step2(receivedUserId, function(receivedUserDetails) { // *Callback for step 2*
    step3(receivedUserDetails, function(receivedPosts) { // *Callback for step
3*
      // *Finally, handle the result of the last step*
      console.log("--- All Steps Complete ---");
      console.log("Final Posts:", receivedPosts);
      console.log("------------------------");
    });
  });
});

console.log("All requests initiated...");
```

Look at the indentation of the callbacks! This deeply nested structure is famously known as the **Pyramid of Doom** or **Callback Hell**.

Why is Callback Hell problematic?

- **Readability**: The code becomes very difficult to read and follow the logical flow.
- **Maintainability**: Adding new steps, modifying existing ones, or changing the order becomes complex and error-prone.
- **Error Handling**: Handling errors consistently across multiple nested callbacks becomes cumbersome. You often need explicit error checks within each callback.

While techniques exist to mitigate callback hell slightly (like naming functions instead of using anonymous ones, or using helper libraries), the fundamental nesting issue remains with the basic callback pattern for sequential asynchronous operations.

Chapter Summary

This chapter introduced the crucial difference between **synchronous** (blocking, one-after-another) and **asynchronous** (non-blocking, happens later) execution in JavaScript. We saw why handling time-consuming operations asynchronously is vital for maintaining a responsive user interface in the browser's single-threaded environment. We used setTimeout as a prime example of a browser API that operates asynchronously. We then defined **callback functions** as the traditional mechanism for handling results or notifications from asynchronous operations once they complete. Finally, we illustrated the significant drawback of relying solely on callbacks for sequential asynchronous tasks: the nesting pattern known as the **Pyramid of Doom** or **Callback Hell**, which hampers readability and maintainability.

Callbacks laid the groundwork for asynchronous programming in JavaScript, but their limitations paved the way for newer, cleaner approaches. In the next chapter, we'll explore **Promises**, a powerful built-in feature designed specifically to manage asynchronous operations more effectively and escape the dreaded Pyramid of Doom.

13
Promises

In the last chapter, we navigated the world of asynchronous operations using callbacks. While functional, we saw how quickly things could get tangled, leading to the infamous "Pyramid of Doom" or "Callback Hell" when dealing with sequential asynchronous tasks. The nested structure made code hard to read, difficult to debug, and prone to errors. Thankfully, JavaScript evolved, and a much cleaner, more robust pattern emerged to handle asynchronous operations: **Promises**. This chapter introduces Promises, explaining what they are, how they work, and how they help us write asynchronous code that is significantly more manageable and readable.

What are Promises?

Think of a Promise like an IOU ("I owe you") slip or a receipt you get when you order something that isn't ready immediately. You don't have the actual item yet, but you have a *promise* that you will eventually receive either the item you ordered (if successful) or a notification explaining why you couldn't get it (if something went wrong).

In JavaScript, a **Promise** is an object that represents the *eventual completion (or failure)* of an asynchronous operation and its resulting value.

Key ideas:

- A Promise acts as a **placeholder** for a value that is not necessarily known when the Promise is created.

- It allows you to associate handlers (callback functions) with an asynchronous action's eventual success value or failure reason.
- It provides a structured way to handle asynchronous results and errors, avoiding deep nesting.

Instead of passing a callback function directly *into* the asynchronous function like we did in Chapter 12 (`fetchUserData(123, displayUserData)`), asynchronous functions that use Promises typically *return* a Promise object immediately. You then attach your success and error handling functions *to this returned Promise object*.

Promise States

A Promise exists in one of three mutually exclusive states:

1. **Pending:** This is the initial state when the Promise is created. The asynchronous operation associated with the Promise has not yet completed or failed. The Promise is "unsettled". Think of this as waiting for your order after getting the receipt.
2. **Fulfilled (or Resolved):** The asynchronous operation completed successfully. The Promise now has a resulting value. The Promise is "settled". Your order is ready and delivered!
3. **Rejected:** The asynchronous operation failed. The Promise now has a reason for the failure (typically an Error object). The Promise is "settled". There was a problem, and they tell you why your order couldn't be completed.

A crucial characteristic of Promises is that once they are "settled" (either fulfilled or rejected), their state and resulting value (or reason) **never change**. A Promise can only succeed or fail once.

Creating Promises (Less Common for Beginners)

While you'll most often *consume* Promises returned by built-in browser APIs (like `fetch`) or third-party libraries, it's helpful to understand how they are created. You use the `Promise` constructor:

```
const myFirstPromise = new Promise((resolve, reject) => {
  // *Inside this function (the "executor"), you perform your async operation*
  console.log("Executor function started... (Async operation begins)");
```

```
  // *Simulate an asynchronous task*
  setTimeout(() => {
    const operationSuccessful = Math.random() > 0.3; // *Simulate
success/failure*

    if (operationSuccessful) {
      const resultValue = "Operation succeeded! Data is here.";
      console.log("Async operation successful. Resolving promise...");
      resolve(resultValue); // *Call resolve() on success, passing the result*
    } else {
      const errorReason = new Error("Operation failed!");
      console.error("Async operation failed. Rejecting promise...");
      reject(errorReason); // *Call reject() on failure, passing the reason*
    }
  }, 1500); // *Simulate 1.5 second delay*
});

console.log("Promise created (currently pending).");
```

The `Promise` constructor takes a single argument: an "executor" function. This executor function itself receives two arguments, which are *functions* provided by the Promise mechanism:

- `resolve(value)`: You call this function when your asynchronous operation completes successfully, passing the resulting `value`. This transitions the Promise from pending to fulfilled.
- `reject(reason)`: You call this function when your asynchronous operation fails, passing the `reason` (usually an Error object). This transitions the Promise from pending to rejected.

Again, you'll typically be *using* Promises returned by functions like `fetch()`, not creating them manually like this very often when starting out.

Consuming Promises

So, you have a Promise object (either one you created or one returned by an API). How do you register the code that should run when the Promise is *fulfilled*? You use the `.then()` method.

```
promise.then(onFulfilled);
```

- promise: The Promise object you want to handle.
- .then(): The method you call on the Promise.
- onFulfilled: A **callback function** that will be executed *if and when* the promise transitions to the fulfilled state. This function automatically receives the Promise's fulfillment value as its single argument.

Let's consume the myFirstPromise we created earlier:

```
console.log("Attaching .then handler to the promise...");

myFirstPromise.then(function handleSuccess(result) {
  // *This function runs ONLY if the promise is fulfilled*
  console.log("--- .then() Handler ---");
  console.log("Promise Fulfilled! Result:", result);
  console.log("----------------------");
});

console.log("Handler attached. Waiting for promise to settle...");

// *Possible Output Scenarios:*

// *Scenario 1 (Promise Fulfilled):*
// Executor function started... (Async operation begins)
// Promise created (currently pending).
// Attaching .then handler to the promise...
// Handler attached. Waiting for promise to settle...
// (after ~1.5 seconds)
// Async operation successful. Resolving promise...
// --- .then() Handler ---
// Promise Fulfilled! Result: Operation succeeded! Data is here.
// ----------------------

// *Scenario 2 (Promise Rejected):*
// Executor function started... (Async operation begins)
// Promise created (currently pending).
// Attaching .then handler to the promise...
// Handler attached. Waiting for promise to settle...
// (after ~1.5 seconds)
// Async operation failed. Rejecting promise...
// *... (error message appears in console, .then handler doesn't run) ...*
```

Notice that the .then() handler only runs if the Promise fulfills. What about handling failures?

Handling Errors

To specify code that should run if a Promise is *rejected*, you use the `.catch()` method.

```
promise.catch(onRejected);
```

- `promise`: The Promise object.
- `.catch()`: The method called on the Promise.
- `onRejected`: A **callback function** executed *if and when* the `promise` transitions to the rejected state. This function receives the rejection reason (usually an Error object) as its argument.

You typically chain `.catch()` after `.then()` (or after a chain of `.then()` calls):

```
myFirstPromise
  .then(function handleSuccess(result) {
    console.log("--- .then() Handler ---");
    console.log("Promise Fulfilled! Result:", result);
    console.log("----------------------");
  })
  .catch(function handleError(error) {
    // *This function runs ONLY if the promise is rejected*
    console.error("--- .catch() Handler ---");
    console.error("Promise Rejected! Reason:", error.message);
    console.error("----------------------");
  });

console.log("Handlers (.then and .catch) attached.");

// *Possible Output Scenarios:*

// *Scenario 1 (Promise Fulfilled):*
// ... (same as before, .then runs, .catch is skipped) ...

// *Scenario 2 (Promise Rejected):*
// Executor function started... (Async operation begins)
// Promise created (currently pending).
// Handlers (.then and .catch) attached.
// (after ~1.5 seconds)
// Async operation failed. Rejecting promise...
// --- .catch() Handler ---
// Promise Rejected! Reason: Operation failed!
// ----------------------
```

Using .catch() provides a centralized place to handle errors that might occur during the asynchronous operation or even within preceding .then() handlers (errors in .then handlers also cause the Promise chain to reject).

Alternative: .then() can actually accept a second argument for the rejection handler: promise.then(onFulfilled, onRejected). However, using .catch() is generally preferred because it makes the code cleaner and handles errors from *both* the original Promise *and* any preceding onFulfilled handlers in the chain.

Cleaning Up

Sometimes, you need to execute a piece of code regardless of whether the Promise was fulfilled or rejected. Common examples include hiding a loading spinner, closing a file, or releasing a resource. The .finally() method is designed for this.

```
promise.finally(onFinally);
```

- onFinally: A callback function that executes when the Promise settles (either fulfilled *or* rejected).
- This function does **not** receive the result value or the rejection reason. Its purpose is purely for cleanup actions that must happen irrespective of the outcome.

```
function simulateOperation() {
  console.log("Starting operation (might succeed or fail)...");
  // *Return the promise from the previous example*
  return new Promise((resolve, reject) => {
    setTimeout(() => {
      if (Math.random() > 0.5) {
        resolve("Data fetched successfully!");
      } else {
        reject(new Error("Network error occurred!"));
      }
    }, 1000);
  });
}

console.log("Showing loading indicator..."); // *Simulate UI action*

simulateOperation()
  .then(result => {
    console.log("Success:", result);
  })
```

```
  .catch(error => {
    console.error("Failure:", error.message);
  })
  .finally(() => {
    // *This runs whether .then or .catch was executed*
    console.log("Hiding loading indicator..."); // *Cleanup action*
    console.log("Operation attempt finished.");
  });
```

The code inside `.finally()` provides a reliable way to perform cleanup.

Chaining Promises for Sequential Operations

This is where Promises truly shine and solve the Callback Hell problem. Both `.then()` and `.catch()` return a **new Promise**. This crucial feature allows us to chain asynchronous operations together in a flat, readable sequence.

Let's rewrite the sequential steps example from Chapter 12 using Promises:

```
// *Assume these functions now return Promises*
function step1Promise() {
  console.log("Step 1: Getting User ID...");
  return new Promise((resolve) => { // *Simplified: only handling success*
    setTimeout(() => {
      const userId = 5;
      console.log("Step 1 Complete. User ID:", userId);
      resolve(userId); // *Fulfill the promise with the userId*
    }, 500);
  });
}

function step2Promise(userId) {
  console.log("Step 2: Fetching Details for User", userId);
  return new Promise((resolve) => {
    setTimeout(() => {
      const userDetails = { name: "Alice", id: userId };
      console.log("Step 2 Complete. Details:", userDetails);
      resolve(userDetails); // *Fulfill with user details*
    }, 500);
  });
}

function step3Promise(userDetails) {
  console.log("Step 3: Fetching Posts for User", userDetails.name);
  return new Promise((resolve) => {
```

```
    setTimeout(() => {
      const posts = ["Post A", "Post B"];
      console.log("Step 3 Complete. Posts:", posts);
      resolve(posts); // *Fulfill with posts*
    }, 500);
  });
}


// --- The Promise Chain ---
console.log("Starting sequential async operations with Promises...");

step1Promise() // *Call step 1, returns a promise*
  .then(receivedUserId => {
    // *The result of step1Promise (userId) is passed here*
    // *Call step 2, passing the userId, and RETURN its promise*
    return step2Promise(receivedUserId);
  })
  .then(receivedUserDetails => {
    // *The result of step2Promise (userDetails) is passed here*
    // *Call step 3, passing userDetails, and RETURN its promise*
    return step3Promise(receivedUserDetails);
  })
  .then(receivedPosts => {
    // *The result of step3Promise (posts) is passed here*
    // *Final handling*
    console.log("--- All Steps Complete (Promises) ---");
    console.log("Final Posts:", receivedPosts);
    console.log("-----------------------------------");
  })
  .catch(error => {
    // *A single .catch handles errors from ANY preceding step*
    console.error("--- An Error Occurred in the Chain ---");
    console.error(error);
    console.error("-------------------------------------");
  });

console.log("All Promises initiated...");
```

Look at the difference! No deep nesting. The code reads almost like a synchronous sequence: do step 1, *then* do step 2 with the result, *then* do step 3 with the result, *then* handle the final result, *and catch* any errors along the way.

How Chaining Works:

1. step1Promise() is called, returning promise1.
2. The first .then(handler1) is attached to promise1.

3. When `promise1` fulfills, `handler1` executes (receiving `userId`).
4. `handler1` calls `step2Promise(userId)`, which returns `promise2`. Crucially, `handler1` **returns** `promise2`.
5. The first `.then()` itself returns a *new* promise, `promiseChainLink1`. This `promiseChainLink1` will adopt the state of `promise2` (the one returned from inside `handler1`).
6. The second `.then(handler2)` is attached to `promiseChainLink1`.
7. When `promise2` (returned by `step2Promise`) fulfills, `promiseChainLink1` also fulfills, causing `handler2` to execute (receiving `userDetails`).
8. This pattern repeats down the chain.
9. If any promise in the chain rejects (e.g., `step2Promise` fails), or if any handler throws an error, the chain skips subsequent `.then` handlers and jumps directly to the nearest `.catch()` handler.

This chaining mechanism, based on `.then` returning promises, is the key to escaping callback hell.

Running Promises in Parallel

What if you have multiple asynchronous tasks that *don't* depend on each other, and you want to run them concurrently and wait for all of them to finish? For instance, fetching data from three different API endpoints. Running them sequentially using `.then` chains would be unnecessarily slow.

`Promise.all()` is the tool for this job.

```
Promise.all(iterableOfPromises);
```

- It takes an iterable (usually an array) of Promises as input.
- It returns a **single new Promise** that behaves as follows:
  - **Fulfills:** When *all* the Promises in the input iterable have fulfilled. The fulfillment value is an **array** containing the fulfillment values of the input Promises, in the same order as they appeared in the input array.
  - **Rejects:** As soon as *any one* of the input Promises rejects. The rejection reason is the reason from the first Promise that rejected.

```
function fetchData(url, delay) {
  return new Promise((resolve) => {
    setTimeout(() => {
      console.log(`Fetched data from ${url}`);
```

```
          resolve(`Data from ${url}`);
      }, delay);
  });
}

const promise1 = fetchData('/api/users', 1000);
const promise2 = fetchData('/api/posts', 500);
const promise3 = fetchData('/api/settings', 1200);

console.log("Initiating parallel fetches...");

Promise.all([promise1, promise2, promise3])
  .then(results => {
    // *'results' is an array: [result from promise1, result from promise2,
result from promise3]*
    console.log("--- All Fetches Complete ---");
    console.log("Results:", results);
    // *Example Output: Results: [ 'Data from /api/users', 'Data from
/api/posts', 'Data from /api/settings' ]*
    console.log("------------------------");
  })
  .catch(error => {
    // *This runs if ANY of the fetchData calls were to reject*
    console.error("--- One of the Fetches Failed ---");
    console.error(error);
    console.error("-----------------------------");
  });

console.log("Promise.all initiated...");
```

`Promise.all` allows you to efficiently manage multiple concurrent asynchronous operations.

Other Promise Combinators (Brief Mention)

Besides `Promise.all()`, JavaScript provides other methods for combining Promises, though they are less commonly needed for beginners:

- `Promise.race(iterable)`: Returns a Promise that settles (fulfills or rejects) as soon as the *first* Promise in the iterable settles.
- `Promise.allSettled(iterable)`: Returns a Promise that fulfills after *all* input Promises have settled (either fulfilled or rejected). The result is an array of objects describing the outcome of each input Promise. Useful when you need to know the result of every operation, even if some failed.

- `Promise.any(iterable)`: Returns a Promise that fulfills as soon as *any one* of the input Promises fulfills. It rejects only if *all* input Promises reject.

Chapter Summary

This chapter introduced **Promises** as a modern, structured way to handle asynchronous operations in JavaScript, providing a significant improvement over the nested callback pattern (Callback Hell). We learned that a Promise is an object representing the eventual outcome (fulfillment or rejection) of an async task, existing in one of three states: **pending**, **fulfilled**, or **rejected**. We saw how to consume Promises using the `.then()` method for success cases, `.catch()` for handling errors, and `.finally()` for cleanup code that runs regardless of the outcome. The real power emerged when we explored **chaining Promises** using `.then()`, which allows for clean, readable sequential asynchronous logic. We also learned how to run multiple independent Promises concurrently and wait for all to complete using `Promise.all()`.

Promises dramatically improve the way we write and reason about asynchronous code. However, even with chaining, the syntax still involves callbacks within `.then()` and `.catch()`. Can we make asynchronous code look almost exactly like synchronous code? Yes! In the next chapter, we'll explore `async` **and** `await`, special keywords built *on top of* Promises that provide an even more intuitive and readable syntax for handling asynchronous operations.

14
Async/Await

In the last chapter, we celebrated the arrival of Promises, a fantastic improvement over nested callbacks for managing asynchronous operations. Promises gave us `.then()` for handling success, `.catch()` for errors, and a way to chain operations cleanly, escaping the dreaded Pyramid of Doom. It was a huge step forward!

However, if you look closely at Promise chains, you'll notice we're still writing functions (callback functions) inside our `.then()` and `.catch()` calls. While much flatter than callback hell, the structure still involves defining what happens *next* inside these handler functions. What if we could write asynchronous code that *looks* almost exactly like the simple, synchronous, line-by-line code we started with, but still behaves asynchronously without blocking?

That's precisely what the `async` and `await` keywords provide. Introduced in ES2017 (ES8), `async`/`await` is syntactic sugar built *on top of* Promises. It doesn't replace Promises; it gives us a more intuitive and readable syntax for working *with* them, especially when dealing with sequences of asynchronous steps. Get ready for asynchronous code that feels remarkably synchronous!

Introducing `async` Functions

The foundation of this new syntax is the `async` keyword. You place `async` right before the `function` keyword (for declarations or expressions) or before the parameter list for arrow functions (which we'll see in Chapter 18).

```
// Async function declaration
async function myAsyncFunction() {
  // ... code ...
  // Can use 'await' inside here
}

// Async function expression
const myAsyncExpression = async function() {
  // ... code ...
  // Can use 'await' inside here
};

// Async arrow function (brief preview)
// const myAsyncArrow = async () => {
//   // ... code ...
//   // Can use 'await' inside here
// };
```

What does adding async do? Two crucial things:

1. **Implicitly Returns a Promise:** An async function *always* returns a Promise.

   - If the async function explicitly returns a value (e.g., return 42;), the Promise it returns will *fulfill* with that value.
   - If the async function throws an error, the Promise it returns will *reject* with that thrown error.
   - If the async function completes without an explicit return or throw, the Promise it returns will fulfill with the value undefined.

2. **Enables** await: The async keyword allows you to use the await keyword *inside* the function's body to pause execution until a Promise settles.

Let's see the implicit Promise return:

```
async function getGreeting() {
  return "Hello from async!"; // *This value fulfills the returned promise*
}

async function failSometimes() {
  if (Math.random() < 0.5) {
    throw new Error("Async function failed!"); // *This error rejects the
returned promise*
  }
  return "Async function succeeded!";
}
```

```
// Calling an async function returns a promise
const greetingPromise = getGreeting();
console.log(greetingPromise); // *Output: Promise { <pending> } (or fulfilled)*

// We consume it using .then() and .catch() just like any other promise
greetingPromise.then(result => {
  console.log("Greeting received:", result); // *Output: Greeting received:
Hello from async!*
});

failSometimes()
  .then(result => console.log("Success:", result))
  .catch(error => console.error("Error caught:", error.message));
  // *Output will vary: either Success: ... or Error caught: ...*
```

So, even without using await yet, async fundamentally changes a function to operate within the Promise ecosystem.

Pausing Execution with await

The real magic happens when you combine async functions with the await keyword. The await operator can *only* be used inside an async function (*Note: Top-level* await *is a newer feature available in specific environments like modules, but we'll focus on its use within* async *functions for now*).

When you place await before an expression that evaluates to a Promise:

1. The execution of the async function is **paused** at that point. It doesn't block the main thread; it just pauses *that specific function's* execution, allowing other code (including UI updates or other asynchronous tasks) to run.
2. It **waits** for the awaited Promise to settle (either fulfill or reject).
3. **If the Promise fulfills:** await returns the fulfilled value. The function then resumes execution from the next line.
4. **If the Promise rejects:** await throws the rejection reason (usually an error object). Execution within the async function immediately stops at the await line and jumps to the nearest catch block if using try...catch (more on this soon), or causes the async function's returned Promise to reject with that reason.

```
// *A function that returns a promise after a delay*
function resolveAfterDelay(value, delay) {
  return new Promise(resolve => {
```

```
    setTimeout(() => {
      console.log(`Resolving with value: ${value}`);
      resolve(value);
    }, delay);
  });
}

// *An async function using await*
async function processData() {
  console.log("processData: Starting...");

  // *Pause here until the first promise fulfills*
  const result1 = await resolveAfterDelay("Data A", 1000);
  console.log(`processData: Received result 1: ${result1}`);

  // *Pause here until the second promise fulfills*
  const result2 = await resolveAfterDelay("Data B", 500);
  console.log(`processData: Received result 2: ${result2}`);

  // *Pause here until the third promise fulfills*
  const result3 = await resolveAfterDelay("Data C", 800);
  console.log(`processData: Received result 3: ${result3}`);

  console.log("processData: All steps complete.");
  return `Final result: ${result1}, ${result2}, ${result3}`; // *Fulfills the
promise returned by processData*
}

console.log("Calling processData...");
processData()
  .then(finalResult => {
    console.log("--- processData Promise Fulfilled ---");
    console.log(finalResult);
    console.log("--------------------------------");
  });
console.log("processData called, main script continues...");

// *Expected Output Order:*
// Calling processData...
// processData: Starting...
// processData called, main script continues...
// (after ~1 second)
// Resolving with value: Data A
// processData: Received result 1: Data A
// (after ~0.5 seconds more)
// Resolving with value: Data B
// processData: Received result 2: Data B
```

```
// (after ~0.8 seconds more)
// Resolving with value: Data C
// processData: Received result 3: Data C
// processData: All steps complete.
// --- processData Promise Fulfilled ---
// Final result: Data A, Data B, Data C
// ----------------------------------
```

Look how the `processData` function reads almost like synchronous code! `await`
makes it seem like we're just assigning results directly to variables, but under the
hood, it's pausing and waiting for Promises to resolve without blocking.

Writing Cleaner Asynchronous Logic

Now, let's revisit the sequential operation example from the Promises chapter (step 1,
step 2, step 3) and rewrite it using async/await. We'll assume the `step1Promise`,
`step2Promise`, and `step3Promise` functions (which return Promises) are already
defined as before.

```
async function runAllSteps() {
  try { // *We'll discuss try...catch next*
    console.log("Starting sequential async operations with async/await...");

    // *Wait for step 1 and get its result*
    const userId = await step1Promise();

    // *Wait for step 2 (using userId) and get its result*
    const userDetails = await step2Promise(userId);

    // *Wait for step 3 (using userDetails) and get its result*
    const posts = await step3Promise(userDetails);

    // *All steps completed successfully*
    console.log("--- All Steps Complete (async/await) ---");
    console.log("Final Posts:", posts);
    console.log("------------------------------------");

    return posts; // *Return final result (fulfills the promise returned by
runAllSteps)*

  } catch (error) {
    // *Catch errors from ANY of the awaited promises*
    console.error("--- An Error Occurred (async/await) ---");
    console.error(error);
```

```
        console.error("--------------------------------------");
        // *Optionally re-throw or return an error indicator*
        // throw error; // *Rejects the promise returned by runAllSteps*
    }
}

// *Call the async function and handle its resulting promise*
runAllSteps()
    .then(finalPosts => {
        if(finalPosts) { // *Check if execution succeeded*
            console.log("runAllSteps finished successfully.");
        }
    })
    .catch(err => {
        console.error("runAllSteps promise was rejected overall.");
    });

console.log("runAllSteps function called...");
```

Compare the `runAllSteps` function body to the `.then()` chain from Chapter 13. The async/await version is significantly cleaner and more closely resembles standard synchronous code flow. The logic is much easier to follow: get the user ID, then get the details, then get the posts.

Error Handling with `try...catch`

How do we handle rejected Promises when using `await`? Remember that if an awaited Promise rejects, `await` *throws* that rejection reason. We can catch these thrown errors using standard synchronous `try...catch` blocks within our async function!

```
async function potentiallyFailingOperation() {
  return new Promise((resolve, reject) => {
    setTimeout(() => {
      if (Math.random() < 0.5) {
        reject(new Error("Something went wrong randomly!"));
      } else {
        resolve("Operation was successful!");
      }
    }, 1000);
  });
}

async function processWithTryCatch() {
  console.log("Attempting operation...");
```

```
    try {
      // *await the potentially failing operation*
      const result = await potentiallyFailingOperation();

      // *This code only runs if the promise fulfilled*
      console.log("Try block: Success!");
      console.log("Result:", result);
      return result;

    } catch (error) {
      // *This block runs if the awaited promise rejected*
      console.error("Catch block: An error occurred!");
      console.error("Error details:", error.message);
      // *We can handle the error here, maybe return a default value or log it*
      return "Processed with error."; // *Fulfills the outer promise despite the
inner error*
      // Or re-throw if you want the outer promise to reject: throw error;
    } finally {
        // *Optional: Runs whether try or catch executed*
        console.log("Finally block: Operation attempt finished.");
    }
}

processWithTryCatch()
   .then(outcome => console.log("Overall outcome:", outcome))
   .catch(err => console.error("Overall error (if finally re-threw):", err));
```

Using `try...catch` within async functions feels very natural for developers accustomed to synchronous error handling. It allows you to handle errors from awaited Promises in the same way you'd handle errors thrown by regular synchronous code. This contrasts with the `.catch()` method used in Promise chains.

async/await vs. Promises

It's crucial to remember that `async/await` is **built upon Promises**. It doesn't replace them; it provides a different syntax for consuming them.

- **Readability**: `async/await` generally wins for sequential asynchronous operations, making code look flatter and more synchronous.
- **Error Handling**: `try...catch` in async functions often feels more natural than `.catch()` chaining for developers familiar with synchronous error handling.

- **Debugging**: Stepping through `async`/`await` code in debuggers can sometimes feel more straightforward than stepping through Promise chains with multiple callbacks.
- **Underlying Mechanism**: You still need to understand Promises because async functions return them, `await` waits for them, and you'll often interact with APIs or libraries that return Promises directly. `Promise.all()`, `Promise.race()`, etc., are still used within async functions to handle concurrency.

```
// *Using Promise.all within an async function*
async function fetchParallelData() {
  console.log("Fetching user and settings data in parallel...");
  try {
    const results = await Promise.all([
      resolveAfterDelay("User Data", 800),  // *Simulated fetch 1*
      resolveAfterDelay("Settings Data", 600) // *Simulated fetch 2*
    ]);

    // 'results' is an array: ["User Data", "Settings Data"]
    console.log("Parallel fetches complete:", results);
    const userData = results[0];
    const settingsData = results[1];
    // *Process data...*
    return { user: userData, settings: settingsData };

  } catch (error) {
    console.error("Error during parallel fetch:", error);
    throw error; // *Propagate the error*
  }
}

fetchParallelData()
    .then(data => console.log("Final parallel data:", data))
    .catch(err => console.error("fetchParallelData failed."));
```

Choose the approach (`.then`/`.catch` or `async`/`await`) that makes your code clearest for the specific task. Often, `async`/`await` is preferred for coordinating multiple asynchronous steps, while simple `.then`/`.catch` might suffice for handling a single Promise.

Chapter Summary

This chapter introduced the powerful `async` and `await` keywords, which provide syntactic sugar over Promises to make asynchronous code look and feel more synchronous. We learned that the `async` keyword modifies a function so it implicitly returns a Promise and enables the use of `await` inside it. The `await` keyword pauses the execution of an `async` function until a specified Promise settles, returning the fulfilled value or throwing the rejection reason. We saw how this combination dramatically improves the readability of sequential asynchronous operations compared to `.then()` chaining. We also learned how to handle errors from awaited Promises naturally using standard `try...catch` blocks. While `async/await` offers a cleaner syntax, we emphasized that it's built upon Promises, and understanding Promises remains essential.

You now have the most modern and often most readable tools for managing asynchronous operations in JavaScript. However, even with the best asynchronous patterns, errors can still occur – network requests might fail, data might be invalid, or unexpected situations might arise in your logic. In the next chapter, we'll broaden our focus on **Error Handling**, looking at the `try...catch...finally` statement in more general terms and discussing strategies for making your applications more robust and resilient to unexpected problems.

15

Error Handling

Throughout our journey, we've been building programs that, ideally, run smoothly from start to finish. We learned to handle asynchronous operations with Promises and `async`/`await` (Chapters 13 and 14) to prevent blocking. But the reality of software development is that things don't always go according to plan. Networks can fail, users might enter invalid data, servers might return unexpected responses, or we might simply make mistakes in our own code (yes, it happens to everyone!).

Ignoring these potential problems leads to fragile applications that crash, behave unpredictably, or provide a frustrating user experience. Robust, professional applications need to anticipate and gracefully handle errors when they occur. This chapter focuses on JavaScript's primary mechanisms for **error handling**, allowing you to catch problems, react appropriately, and keep your application running smoothly even when the unexpected happens.

Why Error Handling Matters

Imagine using an online shopping site. You click "Add to Cart," but due to a temporary network glitch, the request fails. What should happen?

- **Bad Scenario (No Error Handling):** The JavaScript code might crash, the "loading" spinner keeps spinning forever, or nothing happens, leaving you confused and unable to proceed.

- **Good Scenario (With Error Handling):** The application catches the network error, stops the spinner, and displays a helpful message like, "Oops! Couldn't add the item to your cart. Please check your connection and try again."

Proper error handling is crucial for:

- **User Experience:** Prevents abrupt crashes and provides informative feedback, guiding the user.
- **Application Stability:** Allows the application to recover from non-fatal errors and continue running where possible.
- **Data Integrity:** Helps prevent actions based on incorrect or incomplete data resulting from an error.
- **Debugging:** Makes it easier to identify *where* and *why* things went wrong during development by catching and logging errors.

The `try...catch` **Statement**

The cornerstone of synchronous error handling in JavaScript (and also for handling errors from `await` expressions) is the `try...catch` statement. It allows you to "try" running a block of code that might potentially cause an error, and "catch" that error if it occurs, preventing it from crashing your program.

The basic syntax looks like this:

```
try {
  // Code that might potentially throw an error
  // (e.g., risky operations, code using await)
} catch (error) {
  // Code to execute ONLY if an error occurred in the 'try' block
  // The 'error' variable holds information about the error
}
// Code here continues execution whether an error was caught or not
```

How it Works:

1. The code inside the `try` block is executed first.
2. **If no error occurs** within the `try` block, the entire `catch` block is skipped, and execution continues with the code immediately following the `try...catch` statement.
3. **If an error** *does* **occur** at any point within the `try` block:
   - The execution of the `try` block stops *immediately* at the line where the error occurred.

- The JavaScript engine looks for the nearest enclosing `catch` block.
- If found, control jumps to the beginning of that `catch` block.
- An **error object**, containing details about the error, is automatically created and passed as an argument to the `catch` block (we've named it `error` here, but you can use any valid variable name).
- The code inside the `catch` block executes, allowing you to handle the error (e.g., log it, display a message).
- After the `catch` block finishes, execution continues with the code *after* the `try...catch` statement (unless the `catch` block itself throws another error or uses `return`).

Example: Handling a Potential Synchronous Error

```
let userProfile = null; // *Imagine this wasn't loaded correctly*

try {
  console.log("Attempting to access user name...");
  // *This line will cause an error because userProfile is null*
  let userName = userProfile.name;
  console.log(`Welcome, ${userName}!`); // *This line will NOT be reached*
} catch (error) {
  console.error("--- An Error Occurred! ---");
  console.error("Failed to access user profile property.");
  // *Inspect the error object*
  console.error("Error Type:", error.name);     // *Output: TypeError*
  console.error("Error Message:", error.message); // *e.g., "Cannot read
properties of null (reading 'name')*
  // console.error("Stack Trace:", error.stack); // *Detailed call stack*
  console.error("-------------------------");
  // *Provide fallback behavior or user feedback*
  console.log("Displaying generic welcome message instead.");
}

console.log("Program continues after try...catch.");

// *Output:*
// Attempting to access user name...
// --- An Error Occurred! ---
// Failed to access user profile property.
// Error Type: TypeError
// Error Message: Cannot read properties of null (reading 'name')
// -------------------------
// Displaying generic welcome message instead.
// Program continues after try...catch.
```

Without try...catch, the TypeError would have stopped the entire script. Here, we caught it and allowed the program to continue.

Using with await (Recap from Chapter 14)

As we saw, try...catch is also the standard way to handle rejected Promises when using await:

```
async function fetchData() {
  try {
    console.log("Fetching data...");
    const responsePromise = someApiThatReturnsAPromise(); // *Assume this
exists*
    const data = await responsePromise; // *If responsePromise rejects, await
throws*
    console.log("Data received:", data);
    // *Process data...*
  } catch (error) {
    console.error("Failed to fetch data:", error.message);
    // *Handle the asynchronous error*
  }
}
```

The catch block will catch errors thrown by the await expression if the awaited Promise rejects.

The finally Block

Sometimes, there's cleanup code you need to run *after* the try block (and potentially the catch block) finishes, regardless of whether an error occurred or not. Common examples include closing network connections, releasing file handles (more common in Node.js), or hiding a loading spinner that was shown before the try block.

The finally block is designed for exactly this purpose. It's added after the catch block.

```
try {
  // Risky code
} catch (error) {
  // Error handling code
} finally {
  // Cleanup code - ALWAYS executes after try/catch completes
}
```

Execution Flow with `finally`:

1. try block executes.
2. If no error: try completes -> `finally` executes -> code after `finally` executes.
3. If an error occurs: try stops -> `catch` executes -> `finally` executes -> code after `finally` executes.
4. If an error occurs and there's no `catch`, or the `catch` block itself throws an error: try stops -> (catch might run and throw) -> `finally` executes -> the error propagates outwards (program might stop if not caught elsewhere).

The `finally` block is guaranteed to run (unless the entire program terminates abruptly), making it ideal for essential cleanup.

Example:

```
let resourceAcquired = false;

try {
  console.log("Acquiring resource...");
  resourceAcquired = true; // *Simulate getting a resource*
  console.log("Resource acquired. Performing operation...");

  // *Simulate potential error during operation*
  if (Math.random() < 0.5) {
    throw new Error("Operation failed mid-way!");
  }

  console.log("Operation completed successfully.");

} catch (error) {
  console.error("Caught an error during operation:", error.message);
  // *Handle specific error...*

} finally {
  // *This cleanup runs whether the operation succeeded or failed*
  console.log("Entering finally block...");
  if (resourceAcquired) {
    console.log("Releasing resource...");
    resourceAcquired = false; // *Simulate cleanup*
  } else {
      console.log("No resource was acquired, nothing to release.");
  }
  console.log("Finally block finished.");
}

console.log("Execution continues after try...catch...finally.");
```

Throwing Your Own Errors

So far, we've mostly focused on *catching* errors that JavaScript or external operations might generate. But sometimes, *your own code* needs to signal that something is wrong based on your application's logic. Perhaps a function receives invalid input, or an essential condition isn't met.

You can generate your own errors using the `throw` statement. When `throw` is executed, it immediately stops the current execution flow (just like a built-in error would) and starts the process of looking for an enclosing `catch` block.

```
throw expression;
```

The `expression` you throw can technically be any value (a string, a number, a boolean), but it's **strongly recommended** to always throw an `Error` object (or an object inheriting from `Error`).

```
function calculateDiscount(price, percentage) {
  if (typeof price !== 'number' || price <= 0) {
    // *Throw an error for invalid input*
    throw new Error("Invalid price provided. Price must be a positive number.");
  }
  if (typeof percentage !== 'number' || percentage < 0 || percentage > 100) {
    throw new Error("Invalid percentage. Must be between 0 and 100.");
  }

  return price - (price * (percentage / 100));
}

try {
  let discountedPrice = calculateDiscount(50, 10); // *Valid input*
  console.log(`Discounted Price 1: ${discountedPrice}`);

  discountedPrice = calculateDiscount(-5, 10); // *Invalid price*
  console.log(`Discounted Price 2: ${discountedPrice}`); // *This won't run*

} catch (error) {
  console.error("Error calculating discount:", error.message);
}

try {
    let discountedPrice3 = calculateDiscount(100, 150); // *Invalid percentage*
    console.log(`Discounted Price 3: ${discountedPrice3}`); // *This won't run*
} catch (error) {
```

```
      console.error("Error calculating discount:", error.message);
}

// *Output:*
// Discounted Price 1: 45
// Error calculating discount: Invalid price provided. Price must be a positive
number.
// Error calculating discount: Invalid percentage. Must be between 0 and 100.
```

Throwing specific errors makes your functions more robust by clearly indicating when preconditions are not met, preventing them from proceeding with invalid data.

The `Error` Object

As mentioned, it's best practice to throw instances of the built-in `Error` object or its descendants. Creating one is simple:

```
const myError = new Error("A descriptive message about what went wrong");
```

Why use `Error` objects?

- **Standard Properties:** They come with standard properties that error handling tools and developers expect:
  - `error.name`: A string indicating the type of error (e.g., "Error", "TypeError", "ReferenceError"). For standard errors, this is set automatically. For `new Error()`, it defaults to "Error".
  - `error.message`: The descriptive string you passed to the constructor.
  - `error.stack` (non-standard but widely supported): A string containing the stack trace – the sequence of function calls that led up to the error. This is incredibly useful for debugging.
- **Clarity:** Using `instanceof Error` in a `catch` block can help differentiate between intentionally thrown errors and other potential exceptions.
- **Built-in Error Types:** JavaScript has several built-in error constructors that inherit from `Error`, representing specific categories of errors:
  - `SyntaxError`: Code violates JavaScript's syntax rules (usually caught by the engine *before* execution).
  - `ReferenceError`: Trying to access a variable that hasn't been declared.
  - `TypeError`: An operation is performed on a value of an inappropriate type (e.g., calling a method on `null`, treating a string like a function).

- `RangeError`: A number is outside its allowed range (e.g., invalid array length).
- `URIError`: Problem encoding or decoding a URI.

You can use these more specific error types when throwing your own errors if they fit the situation:

```
function accessArray(arr, index) {
    if (index < 0 || index >= arr.length) {
        throw new RangeError(`Index ${index} is out of bounds for array of
length ${arr.length}`);
    }
    return arr[index];
}

try {
    let colors = ["red", "green"];
    console.log(accessArray(colors, 1)); // *Output: green*
    console.log(accessArray(colors, 5)); // *Throws RangeError*
} catch (error) {
    console.error(`Caught Error: ${error.name} - ${error.message}`);
    // *Output: Caught Error: RangeError - Index 5 is out of bounds for array of
length 2*
}
```

Error Handling Strategies

Okay, we know *how* to catch and throw errors, but *where* and *how* should we apply this?

- **Be Specific:** Catch errors as close as possible to where they might occur if you can handle them meaningfully there. Avoid overly broad `try...catch` blocks around large chunks of code unless it's for general top-level logging.
- **Don't Swallow Errors:** Avoid empty `catch` blocks (`catch (error) {}`). At the very least, log the error (`console.error(error)`) so you know something went wrong during development. Silently ignoring errors makes debugging nearly impossible.
- **User Feedback:** Don't show raw technical error messages (`error.message`, `error.stack`) directly to end-users. Catch the technical error, log it for yourself, and display a user-friendly message explaining the problem in simple terms and suggesting solutions if possible.

- **Promises:** Remember that .catch() is the idiomatic way to handle errors in Promise chains, though try...catch with await achieves the same goal within async functions.
- **Cleanup:** Use finally for code that *must* run to clean up resources, regardless of success or failure.

Chapter Summary

This chapter equipped you with the essential tools for **Error Handling** in JavaScript. We learned that anticipating and managing errors is crucial for creating robust and user-friendly applications. We explored the fundamental try...catch statement for handling synchronous errors and errors thrown by await. We saw how the optional finally block provides a reliable mechanism for executing cleanup code. We learned how to signal problems in our own logic by **throwing** custom errors using the throw statement, emphasizing the best practice of throwing instances of the built-in Error object (or its descendants like TypeError, RangeError) to provide standardized error information (name, message, stack). Finally, we touched upon practical strategies for applying these tools effectively.

With the ability to handle errors gracefully and manage asynchronous operations effectively, our code is becoming much more resilient. However, as applications grow, keeping all our code – functions, variables, object definitions – in a single file becomes impractical. We need ways to organize our code into logical, reusable units. In the next chapter, we'll explore **Modules**, JavaScript's system for splitting code across multiple files and sharing functionality between them.

16
Modules

As our JavaScript applications grow in complexity, adding more functions, objects, variables, and logic, keeping everything in a single `.js` file becomes increasingly difficult. Imagine a book where every single word, sentence, and paragraph from every chapter was written sequentially in one enormous scroll – finding specific information, making edits, or rearranging sections would be a nightmare! Similarly, large JavaScript projects crammed into one file suffer from:

- **Poor Readability:** It's hard to navigate and understand the overall structure.
- **Naming Collisions:** Different parts of the code might accidentally use the same variable or function names, leading to unexpected overwrites and bugs (especially polluting the global scope, as we discussed in Chapter 9).
- **Difficult Maintenance:** Changing one piece of logic might unintentionally break another unrelated part.
- **Lack of Reusability:** Extracting a useful function or component for use in another project becomes a tedious copy-paste exercise.

We need a way to break our code down into smaller, self-contained, logical units. This is where **Modules** come in. Modules allow you to split your JavaScript code across multiple files, keeping related functionality together. Each module can then choose which parts of its code (variables, functions, classes, etc.) to make available for other modules to use (`export`) and which modules it needs to rely on (`import`). This chapter explores the standard module system built into modern JavaScript, known as ES Modules (ECMAScript Modules).

The Need for Modules

Before ES Modules became the standard, the JavaScript community devised various patterns and systems to tackle the problem of code organization:

- **The Module Pattern (using IIFEs):** Involved wrapping code in Immediately Invoked Function Expressions (IIFEs) to create private scope and selectively exposing public interfaces. While clever, it relied on conventions and could be verbose.
- **Asynchronous Module Definition (AMD):** Popularized by RequireJS, used primarily in browsers for asynchronously loading modules.
- **CommonJS (CJS):** The module system traditionally used by Node.js on the server-side, using `require()` to import and `module.exports` to export.

While you might encounter these older systems (especially CommonJS in Node.js environments or legacy code), **ES Modules (ESM)** is the official, standardized module system specified by ECMAScript and supported natively by modern browsers and Node.js. ESM provides a cleaner, declarative syntax built directly into the language. This chapter focuses exclusively on ES Modules.

ES Modules (ESM)

The core principles of ES Modules are straightforward:

1. **File-Based:** Each file (`.js`) is treated as a separate module.
2. **Module Scope:** Variables, functions, and classes declared at the top level within a module file are **local** to that module by default. They are not automatically added to the global scope.
3. **Explicit Exports:** To make something defined within a module accessible to other modules, you must explicitly **export** it using the `export` keyword.
4. **Explicit Imports:** To use functionality exported by another module, you must explicitly **import** it into your current module using the `import` keyword.
5. **Strict Mode:** Module code automatically runs in JavaScript's strict mode (which helps catch common errors and enforces stricter syntax) without needing `"use strict";`.

This system promotes encapsulation, prevents global scope pollution, and makes dependencies clear.

Exporting Code

Let's imagine we have a file named `utils.js` where we define some helper functions. We need to export them so other files can use them.

Named Exports

You can export multiple values from a module by name. There are two ways to do this:

1. Inline Exports: Place the `export` keyword directly before the declaration of the variable, function, or class you want to export.

```
// File: utils.js

export const PI = 3.14159;

export function calculateCircumference(radius) {
  return 2 * PI * radius;
}

export function calculateArea(radius) {
  return PI * radius * radius;
}

// *This function is NOT exported, it's local to utils.js*
function logCalculation(value) {
  console.log("Calculated value:", value);
}
```

2. Export List: Declare your items normally, then list the ones you want to export in an `export` statement at the end of the file (or anywhere at the top level). You can also rename exports using the as keyword.

```
// File: config.js

const apiKey = "xyz123abc";
const defaultTimeout = 5000; // *milliseconds*

function connectToApi() {
  console.log(`Connecting with API key: ${apiKey}`);
  // ... connection logic ...
}
```

```
// *Export specific items at the end*
export { apiKey, defaultTimeout as timeoutDuration, connectToApi };

// *apiKey is exported as 'apiKey'*
// *defaultTimeout is exported as 'timeoutDuration'*
// *connectToApi is exported as 'connectToApi'*
```

Named exports allow consumers of your module to import only the specific pieces they need.

Default Exports

Sometimes, a module is primarily designed to export one main thing, like a class definition or a main configuration object. For this, you can use a **default export**. A module can have **at most one** default export.

```
// File: UserProfile.js

// *Exporting a class as the default*
export default class UserProfile {
  constructor(name, email) {
    this.name = name;
    this.email = email;
  }

  displayInfo() {
    console.log(`Name: ${this.name}, Email: ${this.email}`);
  }
}

// *You could also export a function or value as default:*
// export default function sayHello() { ... }
// export default { theme: 'dark', fontSize: 12 };
```

You don't use a name immediately after `export default` (unless exporting an already declared named function or class). The importing module gets to choose the name when importing the default value.

Note: While you *can* combine named exports and a default export in the same module, it's often clearer to stick primarily to one style (mostly named or mostly default) within a single module if possible.

Importing Code

Now, let's say we have another file, `main.js`, and we want to use the functionality exported from `utils.js`, `config.js`, and `UserProfile.js`. We use the `import` statement at the top of `main.js`.

Importing Named Exports

To import values that were exported by name, you use curly braces {} listing the specific names you want.

```
// File: main.js

// *Import specific named exports from utils.js*
import { calculateArea, calculateCircumference, PI } from './utils.js';

// *Import named exports from config.js, using the exported alias*
import { apiKey, timeoutDuration } from './config.js';

console.log(`PI is approximately: ${PI}`);
let radius = 5;
let area = calculateArea(radius);
let circumference = calculateCircumference(radius);

console.log(`Radius: ${radius}, Area: ${area}, Circumference: $
{circumference}`);
console.log(`Using API Key: ${apiKey}, Timeout: ${timeoutDuration}ms`);

// *Attempting to use non-exported items will fail:*
// logCalculation(area); // Error: logCalculation is not defined
```

Renaming Imports: If the imported name conflicts with an existing variable in your current module, or if you simply prefer a different name, you can rename imports using as.

```
// File: main.js (alternative import)
import { calculateArea as computeCircleArea, PI as circleConstant } from
'./utils.js';

let radius = 10;
let area = computeCircleArea(radius); // *Use the new name*
console.log(`Circle Constant: ${circleConstant}, Area: ${area}`);
```

Namespace Import: If you want to import *all* named exports from a module as properties of a single object, you can use the namespace import syntax (`* as ModuleName`).

```
// File: main.js (alternative import)
import * as Utils from './utils.js'; // *Import everything into the 'Utils'
object*
import * as Config from './config.js';

let radius = 2;
let area = Utils.calculateArea(radius); // *Access via Utils.calculateArea*
let circumference = Utils.calculateCircumference(radius);
console.log(`Radius: ${radius}, Area: ${area}, Circumference: $
{circumference}`);
console.log(`Config API Key: ${Config.apiKey}`);
```

Importing Default Exports

When importing a default export, you don't use curly braces. You simply provide a name (which can be anything you choose) for the imported value.

```
// File: main.js (continued)

// *Import the default export from UserProfile.js*
// *We can choose any name here, 'UserProfile' is conventional*
import UserProfile from './UserProfile.js';

const user1 = new UserProfile("Bob", "bob@example.com");
user1.displayInfo(); // *Output: Name: Bob, Email: bob@example.com*
```

Importing Both Default and Named Exports

If a module provides both a default export and named exports, you can import them together in a single statement. The default import comes first, followed by the named imports in curly braces.

```
// *Assuming 'moduleX.js' has: export default function main() {...}*
// *and: export const version = '1.0';*

import mainAction, { version } from './moduleX.js';

console.log(`Running module version: ${version}`);
mainAction();
```

File Paths

The string following the `from` keyword specifies the path to the module file.

- **Relative Paths:** Paths starting with `./` (current directory) or `../` (parent directory) are relative to the location of the *current* module file. This is the most common way to link your own project modules.
  - `'./utils.js'`
  - `'../components/Button.js'`
- **Absolute Paths:** Paths starting with `/` relate to the root of the domain (less common for module imports).
- **Bare Specifiers:** Module names that don't start with `.`, `..`, or `/` (e.g., `'lodash'` or `'react'`). These typically refer to external libraries installed via a package manager (like npm) and require specific configuration or build tools to resolve correctly. We won't delve into package management here.

File Extensions: In browsers, you generally **must** include the `.js` file extension (or `.mjs` in some contexts) in your import paths. Node.js has rules that sometimes allow omitting the extension, but being explicit is often safer.

Modules in HTML (`<script type="module">`)

To use ES Modules directly in a web browser, you need to tell the browser that your script file *is* a module. You do this by adding the `type="module"` attribute to your `<script>` tag in the HTML file.

```
<!DOCTYPE html>
<html>
<head>
    <title>Using Modules</title>
    <!-- CSS, etc. -->
</head>
<body>
    <h1>My Modular App</h1>
    <!-- Content -->

    <!-- Load the main entry point script as a module -->
    <script type="module" src="main.js"></script>

    <!-- You can also have inline module scripts -->
```

```
    <!-- <script type="module">
      import { someFunction } from './otherModule.js';
      someFunction();
    </script> -->
</body>
</html>
```

Key behaviors of `<script type="module">`:

- **Enables** `import/export`: Allows the use of ES Module syntax within the script and any modules it imports.
- **Deferred Execution:** Module scripts behave like scripts with the `defer` attribute by default. They are downloaded potentially in parallel, but executed only *after* the HTML document has been fully parsed, maintaining their relative order.
- **Module Scope:** Top-level variables declared in a module script are local to that script, not global.
- **Strict Mode:** Enabled by default.

Structuring Projects with Modules

Modules naturally encourage better project organization:

- **Separation of Concerns:** Group related functions, classes, or data into their own files (e.g., `apiClient.js`, `domUtils.js`, `userValidation.js`).
- **Directories:** Use directories to group related modules (e.g., `src/components/`, `src/helpers/`, `src/services/`).
- **Clear Dependencies:** `import` statements at the top of a file clearly document what other parts of the system the module relies on.
- **Refactoring:** Modifying the internals of one module is less likely to break others, as long as the exported interface remains consistent.
- **Testing:** Self-contained modules are generally easier to test in isolation.

Module Scope Revisited

It's worth re-emphasizing: declaring a variable or function at the top level inside a file treated as a module *does not* make it global.

```
// File: moduleOne.js
let message = "Hello from Module One"; // *Local to moduleOne.js*
```

```
export function greet() {
  console.log(message);
}

// File: moduleTwo.js
import { greet } from './moduleOne.js';

let message = "Hi from Module Two"; // *Local to moduleTwo.js - NO conflict!*

greet(); // *Output: Hello from Module One*
console.log(message); // *Output: Hi from Module Two*
```

Modules provide true encapsulation, solving the global namespace pollution problem that plagued earlier JavaScript development patterns.

Dynamic Imports (Brief Mention)

While standard `import` statements must be at the top level of a module, there's also a way to load modules dynamically or conditionally using the `import()` function-like syntax. `import(modulePath)` starts loading the module and returns a **Promise** that fulfills with the module's namespace object once loading is complete.

```
// *Load './analytics.js' only if the user clicks a specific button*
const analyticsButton = document.getElementById('trackBtn');

analyticsButton.addEventListener('click', () => {
  import('./analytics.js') // *Returns a Promise*
    .then(AnalyticsModule => {
      // *Module loaded successfully*
      AnalyticsModule.trackEvent('button_click');
    })
    .catch(error => {
      console.error("Failed to load analytics module:", error);
    });
});
```

This is more advanced but essential for techniques like **code splitting** (loading parts of your application only when needed) to improve initial page load performance.

Chapter Summary

This chapter tackled the critical task of organizing larger JavaScript codebases using **ES Modules (ESM)**. We saw how modules solve the problems of global scope pollution and naming collisions by giving each file its own **module scope**. We learned how to make functionality available using `export` (both **named exports** for multiple items and **default exports** for a single primary item) and how to consume that functionality in other modules using `import` (importing by name `{...}`, using aliases `as`, namespace imports `* as Name`, and importing defaults). We covered how to enable modules in the browser using `<script type="module">` and discussed the benefits modules bring to project structure, maintainability, and reusability. We also briefly touched upon dynamic imports with `import()`.

With modules, you can structure your code logically, making it easier to manage, test, and collaborate on. Now that we can organize our code and handle asynchronous operations, we're ready to tackle a common asynchronous task in web development: communicating with servers to fetch or send data using APIs. In the next chapter, we'll explore how to use the `fetch` API to make network requests.

17
Working with APIs

In the previous chapter, we mastered Modules, learning how to organize our code into separate, reusable files. We've also tackled asynchronous operations using Callbacks, Promises, and the elegant `async`/`await` syntax (Chapters 12-14). Now, we're ready to apply these concepts to one of the most common asynchronous tasks in web development: communicating with servers.

Modern web applications rarely exist in isolation. They often need to fetch data from a central source (like product information, user profiles, or news articles), send user input to be saved (like submitting a form or posting a comment), or interact with third-party services (like getting weather information or processing payments). This communication happens over the network, typically between the user's browser (the client) and a remote computer (the server). The rules and contracts that govern how these different software components talk to each other are defined by **Application Programming Interfaces (APIs)**. This chapter introduces you to the world of web APIs and shows you how to use JavaScript's built-in `fetch` API to make network requests and handle the responses, often using the popular JSON data format.

What is an API?

Imagine going to a restaurant. You don't walk into the kitchen and start cooking your own food. Instead, you interact with a **menu** (which lists the available options and what they contain) and a **waiter** (who takes your order, relays it to the kitchen, and brings the food back to you).

In the software world, an **API (Application Programming Interface)** acts like that menu and waiter system. It's a defined set of rules, protocols, and tools that allows different software applications or components to communicate and interact with each other without needing to know the intricate details of their internal workings.

In the context of web development, we often talk about **Web APIs**. These are APIs accessed over the internet using the HTTP protocol (the same protocol your browser uses to load web pages). A server exposes a web API, defining specific **endpoints** (URLs) that the client (like your JavaScript code running in the browser) can send requests to. These requests might ask for data (GET), send new data to be created (POST), update existing data (PUT or PATCH), or delete data (DELETE). The server processes the request and sends back a response, usually containing the requested data or a status confirmation.

Key benefits of using APIs:

- **Abstraction:** The client doesn't need to know *how* the server stores data or performs its internal logic; it just needs to know how to make requests according to the API's rules.
- **Modularity:** Different parts of a system (front-end, back-end, mobile app) can be developed independently as long as they adhere to the API contract.
- **Reusability:** A single API on the server can serve multiple clients (web browsers, mobile apps, other servers).

Understanding REST APIs

While there are different styles of web APIs (like SOAP or GraphQL), a very common and influential architectural style is **REST (Representational State Transfer)**. Many web APIs you'll encounter are designed following REST principles, often referred to as **RESTful APIs**.

Core concepts of REST include:

1. **Resources:** Everything is treated as a resource (e.g., a user, a product, a collection of articles). Each resource is identified by a unique URL (Uniform Resource Locator), also called an endpoint.
   - /api/users (Represents a collection of users)
   - /api/users/123 (Represents a specific user with ID 123)
   - /api/products/45 (Represents a specific product)
2. **HTTP Methods (Verbs):** Standard HTTP methods are used to perform actions (CRUD - Create, Read, Update, Delete) on these resources.
   - GET: Retrieve a resource (e.g., GET /api/users/123 to get user 123's details).
   - POST: Create a new resource (e.g., POST /api/users with user data in the request body to create a new user).
   - PUT: Update/replace an existing resource completely (e.g., PUT /api/users/123 with complete updated user data).
   - PATCH: Partially update an existing resource (e.g., PATCH /api/users/123 with just the email field to update only the email).
   - DELETE: Remove a resource (e.g., DELETE /api/users/123 to delete user 123).
3. **Representations:** Clients interact with representations of resources. When you request /api/users/123, you don't get the actual database record; you get a *representation* of that user's data, commonly in a standard format like JSON.
4. **Statelessness:** Each request from the client to the server must contain all the information needed for the server to understand and process it. The server does not store any client context between requests. (Authentication is often handled via tokens passed in headers).

Understanding these REST concepts helps you interpret API documentation and structure your client-side requests effectively.

Making Requests with the fetch API

Modern browsers provide a powerful and flexible function for making network requests: fetch(). It's Promise-based, making it integrate perfectly with the asynchronous patterns we learned in Chapters 13 and 14 (.then/.catch and async/await).

The basic syntax for a simple GET request is:

```
fetch(resourceUrl) // *Pass the URL of the API endpoint*
  .then(response => {
    // *Handle the initial Response object*
```

```
})
.catch(error => {
  // *Handle network errors*
});
```

- `fetch(resourceUrl)`: Initiates the network request to the specified URL. By default, it performs a `GET` request.
- **Returns a Promise:** Crucially, `fetch()` immediately returns a Promise. This Promise doesn't resolve with the actual data directly. Instead, it resolves with a `Response` object as soon as the server sends back the headers of the response. It rejects only if there's a fundamental network error preventing the request from completing (like a DNS issue or the user being offline).

Let's try fetching some data from a sample public API (JSONPlaceholder is great for testing):

```
const apiUrl = 'https://jsonplaceholder.typicode.com/posts/1'; // *URL for a
single post*

console.log("Initiating fetch request...");

fetch(apiUrl)
  .then(response => {
    // *We get the Response object here, NOT the final data yet*
    console.log("Received initial response:", response);
    // *We need to process the response body to get the data (next step)*
    // *We'll add body processing soon*
  })
  .catch(error => {
    // *This catches network errors ONLY*
    console.error("Fetch failed due to network error:", error);
  });

console.log("Fetch request initiated, waiting for response...");
```

Running this will show you a `Response` object logged in the console, but not the actual post data yet. We need to process the response body.

Handling Responses

The `Response` object that the `fetch` Promise resolves with provides information about the response (like the status code) and methods to read the response body content.

Reading the body is *also* an asynchronous operation because the entire body might not have arrived when the headers did. Therefore, the body-reading methods *also return Promises.*

Key Response properties and methods:

- response.ok: A boolean property that is true if the HTTP status code is in the successful range (200-299) and false otherwise (e.g., for 404 Not Found, 500 Internal Server Error). **This is crucial for checking application-level success.**
- response.status: The numeric HTTP status code (e.g., 200, 404, 503).
- response.statusText: A string corresponding to the status code (e.g., "OK", "Not Found").
- response.headers: A Headers object containing the response headers.
- response.json(): Reads the response body and attempts to parse it as JSON. Returns a Promise that resolves with the resulting JavaScript object or array.
- response.text(): Reads the response body and returns a Promise that resolves with the body as a plain string.
- response.blob(): Reads the response body and returns a Promise that resolves with a Blob object (useful for images, files, binary data).

Now, let's properly handle the response and extract the JSON data:

```
const apiUrl = 'https://jsonplaceholder.typicode.com/posts/1';

console.log("Fetching post data...");

fetch(apiUrl)
  .then(response => {
    console.log("Initial Response Status:", response.status); // *e.g., 200*
    console.log("Response OK?", response.ok); // *e.g., true*

    // *Check if the response status indicates success*
    if (!response.ok) {
      // *If not OK (e.g., 404, 500), throw an error to trigger .catch()*
      throw new Error(`HTTP error! status: ${response.status}`);
    } else {
      // *If OK, asynchronously parse the JSON body*
      // *Return the promise from response.json() for the next .then()*
      return response.json();
    }
  })
  .then(postData => {
    // *This .then receives the parsed JSON data from response.json()*
    console.log("--- Post Data Received ---");
```

```
      console.log("Title:", postData.title);
      console.log("Body:", postData.body);
      console.log("User ID:", postData.userId);
      console.log("------------------------");
    })
    .catch(error => {
      // *Catches both network errors AND the error thrown if response.ok was
  false*
      console.error("Error fetching or processing data:", error);
    });

console.log("Fetch initiated...");
```

This pattern is very common:

1. Call `fetch()`.
2. In the first `.then()`, check `response.ok`.
3. If not ok, `throw new Error()`.
4. If ok, call `response.json()` (or `.text()`, etc.) and `return` its Promise.
5. In the second `.then()`, process the actual data received from the body-parsing method.
6. Use `.catch()` to handle any errors that occurred along the way.

Working with JSON Data

JSON (JavaScript Object Notation) is a lightweight text-based data interchange format. It's easy for humans to read and write and easy for machines (especially JavaScript) to parse and generate. It's the de facto standard for most web APIs.

JSON syntax looks very similar to JavaScript object literals, but with stricter rules:

- Keys **must** be double-quoted strings (`"key"`).
- Values can be strings (double-quoted), numbers, booleans (`true`/`false`), arrays (`[...]`), other JSON objects (`{...}`), or `null`.
- No functions, `undefined`, comments, or trailing commas are allowed.

Example JSON:

```
{
  "productId": "ABC-789",
  "productName": "Wireless Keyboard",
  "price": 75.50,
  "inStock": true,
```

```
  "tags": ["computer", "peripheral", "wireless"],
  "specs": {
    "layout": "QWERTY",
    "color": "Black"
  },
  "reviews": null
}
```

- **Parsing JSON (Server Response -> JS Object)**: As we saw, `response.json()` handles this automatically when using `fetch`. It takes the JSON text from the response body and converts it into a corresponding JavaScript object or array that you can work with directly.

- **Stringifying JSON (JS Object -> JSON String)**: When you need to *send* data to a server in a format it understands (like in the body of a `POST` or `PUT` request), you often need to convert your JavaScript objects or arrays into a JSON string. JavaScript provides the built-in `JSON` object for this:

  - `JSON.stringify(value)`: Takes a JavaScript value (object, array, primitive) and returns its JSON string representation.

  ```
  const userToSend = {
    name: "Charlie",
    email: "charlie@example.com",
    isAdmin: false,
    lastLogin: new Date() // *Dates don't have a direct JSON equivalent*
  };

  const jsonString = JSON.stringify(userToSend);
  console.log(jsonString);
  // *Output (Date will be converted to ISO string):*
  //
  {"name":"Charlie","email":"charlie@example.com","isAdmin":false,"lastLog
  in":"2023-10-27T10:30:00.123Z"}

  // *Note: Properties with undefined values, function values, or Symbols*
  // *are usually omitted by JSON.stringify().*
  ```

Configuring Requests (Method, Headers, Body)

`fetch()` can do much more than just simple GET requests. You can customize the request by passing an optional second argument: an **options object**.

```
fetch(resourceUrl, {
  method: 'POST', // *or 'GET', 'PUT', 'DELETE', 'PATCH', etc.*
  headers: {
    // *Request headers go here*
  },
  body: /* ... Request body data ... */
});
```

Common options include:

- `method`: A string specifying the HTTP method. Defaults to `'GET'`.
- `headers`: An object (or a `Headers` object) specifying request headers. Headers provide additional information about the request (e.g., the type of data being sent, authentication credentials).
  - `'Content-Type'`: Very important when sending data. Tells the server what format the body data is in. For JSON, use `'application/json'`.
  - `'Authorization'`: Often used to send API keys or tokens for authentication (e.g., `'Bearer your_token_here'`).
  - `'Accept'`: Tells the server what content types the client prefers for the response (e.g., `'application/json'`).
- `body`: The data payload to send with the request. Required for methods like POST, PUT, PATCH.
  - Must be a string, `Blob`, `FormData`, or similar data type.
  - When sending JavaScript objects as JSON, you **must** stringify them first using `JSON.stringify()`.

Putting it Together: POST Request Example

Let's simulate sending a new blog post to our JSONPlaceholder API (it won't actually save it, but it will simulate the response).

```
const createPostUrl = 'https://jsonplaceholder.typicode.com/posts';
```

```
const newPostData = {
  title: 'My Awesome New Post',
  body: 'This is the content of my fantastic post using fetch!',
  userId: 10 // *Associate with a user ID*
};

console.log("Sending POST request...");

fetch(createPostUrl, {
  method: 'POST', // *Specify the method*
  headers: {
    // *Tell the server we're sending JSON*
    'Content-Type': 'application/json'
  },
  // *Convert the JS object to a JSON string for the body*
  body: JSON.stringify(newPostData)
})
  .then(response => {
    console.log("POST Response Status:", response.status); // *Should be 201
Created*
    if (!response.ok) {
      // *Check for non-2xx status codes*
      throw new Error(`HTTP error! status: ${response.status}`);
    }
    // *Parse the JSON response (usually the created object with an ID)*
    return response.json();
  })
  .then(createdPost => {
    console.log("--- Post Created Successfully ---");
    console.log("Created Post:", createdPost); // *Will include an ID assigned
by the server*
    console.log("-----------------------------");
  })
  .catch(error => {
    console.error("Error creating post:", error);
  });

console.log("POST request sent...");
```

Error Handling with `fetch`

This is a common point of confusion. Let's reiterate:

1. The Promise returned by `fetch()` itself **only rejects on network errors** (cannot connect, DNS lookup failed, CORS issues enforced by the browser). It does **not** reject automatically for HTTP error status codes like 404 or 500.
2. For application-level errors indicated by HTTP statuses (4xx client errors, 5xx server errors), the `fetch` Promise **fulfills**, providing the `Response` object.
3. You **must** manually check the `response.ok` property (or `response.status`) within your first `.then()` handler to detect these HTTP errors.
4. If `response.ok` is `false`, you should typically `throw new Error(...)` inside that `.then()` to propagate the error down to your `.catch()` block, ensuring consistent error handling for both network and HTTP errors.

```
// *Robust fetch pattern using async/await*
async function getData(url) {
  try {
    const response = await fetch(url);

    if (!response.ok) {
      // *Handle HTTP errors (4xx/5xx)*
      throw new Error(`HTTP Error: ${response.status} ${response.statusText}`);
    }

    const data = await response.json(); // *Parse JSON body*
    return data; // *Return the successful data*

  } catch (error) {
    // *Catch both network errors (from fetch) and thrown HTTP errors*
    console.error("getData failed:", error);
    // *Optionally, re-throw the error if the caller needs to know*
    throw error;
  }
}

// *Usage:*
getData('https://jsonplaceholder.typicode.com/todos/1')
  .then(todo => console.log("TODO:", todo))
  .catch(err => console.error("Failed to get TODO data overall."));

getData('https://jsonplaceholder.typicode.com/todos/invalid-url') // *Will
likely cause 404*
  .then(todo => console.log("Invalid TODO:", todo))
  .catch(err => console.error("Failed to get invalid TODO data overall."));
```

This `async/await` pattern with the explicit `response.ok` check is a very common and robust way to handle `fetch` requests.

Chapter Summary

In this chapter, we explored how JavaScript applications communicate with servers using **APIs**, focusing on the common **RESTful API** style which uses URLs for resources and HTTP methods (GET, POST, PUT, DELETE) for actions. We learned how to make network requests from the browser using the modern, Promise-based `fetch` API. We covered handling the `Response` object returned by `fetch`, checking the status with `response.ok`, and asynchronously reading the response body using methods like `response.json()` and `response.text()`. We discussed **JSON** as the standard data format for APIs and how to parse it (`response.json()`) and create it (`JSON.stringify()`). We learned to configure `fetch` requests with options like `method`, `headers` (especially `Content-Type`), and `body` for sending data. Finally, we clarified the nuances of **error handling** with `fetch`, emphasizing the need to check `response.ok` manually to treat HTTP errors consistently with network errors.

You can now empower your web applications to fetch dynamic data, submit user input, and interact with the wider web. As we near the end of our core JavaScript journey, the next chapter will highlight some other powerful and convenient features added to the language in recent years (often referred to as ES6 and beyond) that make writing JavaScript even more efficient and expressive.

18
Modern JavaScript Features (ES6+)

You've journeyed through the core landscape of JavaScript, from variables and loops to functions, objects, asynchronous operations with Promises, and interacting with the DOM. You now possess a solid understanding of how JavaScript works and how to build interactive web applications. However, JavaScript is not a static language; it's constantly evolving. Since 2015, marked by the significant ECMAScript 2015 (ES6) update, the language has seen numerous additions designed to make development more efficient, expressive, and enjoyable. This chapter shines a spotlight on some of the most impactful modern JavaScript features you'll encounter and want to use in your everyday coding. Think of these as powerful upgrades to your JavaScript toolkit.

Arrow Functions (=>)

One of the most visible and frequently used additions from ES6 is **arrow function** syntax. It provides a more concise way to write function expressions.

Compare a traditional function expression (Chapter 8) with its arrow function equivalent:

```
// Traditional Function Expression
```

```
const multiplyRegular = function(a, b) {
  return a * b;
};

// Arrow Function Equivalent
const multiplyArrow = (a, b) => {
  return a * b;
};

console.log(multiplyRegular(5, 6)); // *Output: 30*
console.log(multiplyArrow(5, 6));   // *Output: 30*
```

Key syntax variations and features:

- **Conciseness:** Replaces the `function` keyword with a "fat arrow" (=>) separating the parameters from the function body.

- **Implicit Return:** If the function body consists of only a *single expression*, you can omit the curly braces {} and the `return` keyword. The result of the expression is returned automatically.

  ```
  // Arrow function with implicit return
  const add = (a, b) => a + b;
  console.log(add(10, 5)); // *Output: 15*

  const double = number => number * 2; // *Parentheses optional for single
  param*
  console.log(double(7)); // *Output: 14*
  ```

- **Single Parameter:** If there's exactly one parameter, the parentheses () around it are optional (as seen in `double` above). If there are zero or multiple parameters, parentheses are required.

  ```
  const logMessage = () => console.log("No parameters here!");
  logMessage(); // *Output: No parameters here!*
  ```

- **Lexical `this` Binding:** This is arguably the **most significant difference** beyond syntax. Arrow functions do **not** have their own `this` context. Instead, they *inherit* the `this` value from their surrounding (lexical) scope – the context where the arrow function was *defined*. This behavior contrasts sharply with regular functions, whose `this` value depends on *how they are called* (as briefly touched upon in Chapter 7 and explored further in scope discussions).

Let's illustrate with an object method and `setTimeout` (a common scenario where this binding causes issues with regular functions):

```
const counter = {
  count: 0,
  delay: 1000,

  // *Method using a regular function inside setTimeout*
  startRegular: function() {
    console.log(`startRegular: Initial count is ${this.count}`); //
*'this' is 'counter'*
    setTimeout(function() {
      // *Inside this regular function callback, 'this' is NOT
'counter'.*
      // *It's often 'window' (in browsers) or undefined (strict mode).*
      console.log(`setTimeout (regular): this.count = $
{this.count}`); // *Likely undefined or error*
      // this.count++; // *This would fail or modify the wrong object*
    }, this.delay);
  },

  // *Method using an arrow function inside setTimeout*
  startArrow: function() {
    console.log(`startArrow: Initial count is ${this.count}`); //
*'this' is 'counter'*
    setTimeout(() => {
      // *Arrow function inherits 'this' from startArrow's scope*
      // *So, 'this' here IS the 'counter' object.*
      console.log(`setTimeout (arrow): this.count = ${this.count}`); //
*Correctly accesses 0*
      this.count++; // *This correctly increments counter.count*
       console.log(`setTimeout (arrow): count incremented to $
{this.count}`);
    }, this.delay);
  }
};

// counter.startRegular();
// *Output might show 'undefined' or throw error for this.count in
callback*

counter.startArrow();
// *Output:*
// startArrow: Initial count is 0
// (after 1 second)
// setTimeout (arrow): this.count = 0
// setTimeout (arrow): count incremented to 1
```

Because arrow functions don't rebind `this`, they solve many common problems previously addressed with techniques like `.bind(this)` or storing `this` in another variable (`const self = this;`). Arrow functions are often the preferred choice for callbacks or methods where you need to retain the surrounding `this` context.

Template Literals (Backticks `` ` ``)

Remember painstakingly concatenating strings and variables using the + operator back in Chapter 2?

```
let city = "London";
let country = "UK";
let population = 9;
// *Old way:*
let descriptionOld = "The city of " + city + ", located in the " + country +
                    ", has a population of over " + population + " million.";
console.log(descriptionOld);
```

ES6 introduced **template literals** (also called template strings), which offer a much cleaner and more readable way to create strings, especially those containing embedded expressions or multiple lines. You create template literals using backticks (`` ` ``) instead of single (') or double (") quotes.

- **String Interpolation:** Inside a template literal, you can embed any valid JavaScript expression (like variables, function calls, or arithmetic operations) directly within the string by enclosing it in `${expression}`.

```
let city = "Tokyo";
let country = "Japan";
let population = 37; // *in millions*

// *Using template literals:*
let descriptionNew =
  `The city of ${city}, located in the ${country}, has a population of
over ${population} million.`;
console.log(descriptionNew);
// *Output: The city of Tokyo, located in the Japan, has a population of
over 37 million.*

let price = 10;
let taxRate = 0.08;
let totalMessage = `Total cost: $${(price * (1 + taxRate)).toFixed(2)}`;
```

```
console.log(totalMessage); // *Output: Total cost: $10.80*
```

This interpolation makes creating dynamic strings much more intuitive than repeated concatenation.

- **Multi-line Strings:** Template literals respect line breaks within the backticks, allowing you to create multi-line strings easily without needing special characters like \n.

```
// *Old way for multi-line strings:*
let multiLineOld = "This is the first line.\n" +
                   "This is the second line.";

// *Using template literals:*
let multiLineNew = `This is the first line.
```

This is the second line. Indentation is also preserved.`;

```
console.log(multiLineNew);
/* Output:
This is the first line.
This is the second line.
    Indentation is also preserved.
*/
```

Template literals significantly enhance string handling in JavaScript.

Destructuring Assignment (Arrays and Objects)

Destructuring is a convenient syntax for extracting values from arrays or properties from objects and assigning them directly into distinct variables. It makes accessing nested data much cleaner.

Array Destructuring

You can unpack values from an array into variables using a syntax that mirrors array literal creation.

```
const coordinates = [10, 25, 50]; // *x, y, z coordinates*

// *Old way:*
// const x = coordinates[0];
// const y = coordinates[1];
// const z = coordinates[2];

// *Using array destructuring:*
const [x, y, z] = coordinates;

console.log(`x: ${x}, y: ${y}, z: ${z}`); // *Output: x: 10, y: 25, z: 50*

// *Skip elements using commas:*
const rgbColor = [255, 128, 0];
const [red, , blue] = rgbColor; // *Skip the middle (green) element*
console.log(`Red: ${red}, Blue: ${blue}`); // *Output: Red: 255, Blue: 0*

// *Using Rest operator (...) to collect remaining elements:*
const scores = [95, 88, 76, 92, 81];
const [firstScore, secondScore, ...remainingScores] = scores;
console.log(`First: ${firstScore}, Second: ${secondScore}`); // *Output: First:
95, Second: 88*
console.log(`Remaining: ${remainingScores}`); // *Output: Remaining: 76,92,81*
// *remainingScores is a new array: [ 76, 92, 81 ]*

// *Default values for missing elements:*
const settings = ["dark"];
const [theme = "light", fontSize = 12] = settings;
console.log(`Theme: ${theme}, Font Size: ${fontSize}`); // *Output: Theme: dark,
Font Size: 12*
```

Object Destructuring

Similarly, you can unpack properties from objects into variables using a syntax that mirrors object literal creation. The variable names must match the object keys by default.

```
const user = {
  id: 42,
  displayName: "Alice",
  email: "alice@example.com",
  accountType: "premium"
};

// *Old way:*
```

```
// const id = user.id;
// const name = user.displayName;
// const userEmail = user.email;

// *Using object destructuring:*
const { id, displayName, email } = user; // *Variable names match keys*

console.log(`ID: ${id}, Name: ${displayName}, Email: ${email}`);
// *Output: ID: 42, Name: Alice, Email: alice@example.com*

// *Renaming variables:* Use 'key: newName' syntax
const { accountType: type, displayName: name } = user;
console.log(`User Name: ${name}, Account Type: ${type}`);
// *Output: User Name: Alice, Account Type: premium*

// *Default values for missing properties:*
const config = { timeout: 5000 };
const { timeout = 1000, retries = 3 } = config;
console.log(`Timeout: ${timeout}, Retries: ${retries}`);
// *Output: Timeout: 5000, Retries: 3*

// *Destructuring nested objects:*
const product = {
  pid: 'P123',
  details: { title: 'Laptop', price: 1200 }
};
const { pid, details: { title, price } } = product;
console.log(`Product ID: ${pid}, Title: ${title}, Price: ${price}`);
// *Output: Product ID: P123, Title: Laptop, Price: 1200*
```

Use Case: Function Parameters

Destructuring is particularly useful for handling options objects passed as arguments to functions.

```
// *Function expects an object with 'url' and optional 'method', 'body'*
function makeRequest({ url, method = 'GET', body = null }) {
  console.log(`Making ${method} request to ${url}`);
  if (body) {
    console.log(`With body: ${JSON.stringify(body)}`);
  }
  // ... fetch logic ...
}

// *Call the function with an object - properties are destructured*
```

```
makeRequest({ url: '/api/users' });
// *Output: Making GET request to /api/users*

makeRequest({
  url: '/api/posts',
  method: 'POST',
  body: { title: 'New Post' }
});
// *Output:*
// Making POST request to /api/posts
// With body: {"title":"New Post"}
```

This makes function signatures cleaner and clarifies expected object properties.

Spread (...) and Rest (...) Operators

The three dots (...) syntax serves two related but distinct purposes, depending on the context: **rest parameters** and **spread syntax**.

Rest Parameters

When used as the *last* parameter in a function definition, ... gathers all remaining arguments passed to the function into a proper **array**. This provides a modern alternative to the older, array-like arguments object.

```
// *Using rest parameters to sum numbers*
function sumAll(...numbers) {
  // 'numbers' is a real array containing all arguments passed
  console.log("Arguments received:", numbers);
  let total = 0;
  for (const num of numbers) { // *Can use array methods like for...of*
    total += num;
  }
  return total;
}

console.log(sumAll(1, 2, 3));
// *Output: Arguments received: [ 1, 2, 3 ]*
// *Output: 6*

console.log(sumAll(10, 20, 30, 40, 50));
// *Output: Arguments received: [ 10, 20, 30, 40, 50 ]*
// *Output: 150*
```

```
console.log(sumAll());
// *Output: Arguments received: []*
// *Output: 0*
```

Rest parameters are clearer and provide a true array, making argument handling more straightforward than the legacy `arguments` object.

Spread Syntax

When used *outside* of function parameter definitions, ... acts as the **spread syntax**. It *expands* an iterable (like an array or string) or object properties into individual elements or key-value pairs.

1. Spreading in Function Calls: Expands an array into individual arguments.

```
const nums = [1, 5, 2];
// *Equivalent to Math.max(1, 5, 2)*
const maxVal = Math.max(...nums);
console.log(`Max value: ${maxVal}`); // *Output: Max value: 5*
```

2. Spreading in Array Literals: Creates new arrays by combining existing arrays or adding elements.

```
const arr1 = ['a', 'b'];
const arr2 = ['c', 'd'];

// *Combine arrays:*
const combined = [...arr1, ...arr2, 'e'];
console.log(combined); // *Output: [ 'a', 'b', 'c', 'd', 'e' ]*

// *Create a shallow copy:*
const arr1Copy = [...arr1];
console.log(arr1Copy); // *Output: [ 'a', 'b' ]*
console.log(arr1Copy === arr1); // *Output: false (it's a new array)*
```

3. Spreading in Object Literals: Creates new objects by copying properties from existing objects (shallow copy) or merging objects. Properties listed later overwrite earlier ones with the same key.

```
const defaults = { theme: 'light', fontSize: 12 };
const userSettings = { theme: 'dark', showToolbar: true };
```

```
// *Merge objects (userSettings overrides defaults.theme)*
const finalSettings = { ...defaults, ...userSettings, fontSize: 14 };

console.log(finalSettings);
// *Output: { theme: 'dark', fontSize: 14, showToolbar: true }*

// *Create a shallow copy:*
const defaultsCopy = { ...defaults };
console.log(defaultsCopy); // *Output: { theme: 'light', fontSize: 12 }*
console.log(defaultsCopy === defaults); // *Output: false (new object)*
```

Spread syntax is incredibly versatile for working with arrays and objects non-destruct-ively (creating new ones instead of modifying originals).

Enhanced Object Literals

ES6 introduced several shorthand syntaxes for defining object literals, making them more concise.

- **Shorthand Property Names**: If the variable name holding the value is the same as the desired object key, you can omit the colon and value.

```
let name = "Widget";
let price = 99.99;

// *Old way:*
// const itemOld = { name: name, price: price };

// *Shorthand property names:*
const itemNew = { name, price };
console.log(itemNew); // *Output: { name: 'Widget', price: 99.99 }*
```

- **Shorthand Method Names**: You can omit the function keyword and the colon when defining methods inside an object literal.

```
// *Old way:*
// const calculatorOld = {
//   add: function(a, b) { return a + b; },
//   subtract: function(a, b) { return a - b; }
// };

// *Shorthand method names:*
const calculatorNew = {
```

```
    add(a, b) { return a + b; },
    subtract(a, b) { return a - b; }
  };
  console.log(calculatorNew.add(10, 5)); // *Output: 15*
```

- **Computed Property Names:** Allows you to use an expression (evaluated to a string) as a property key directly within the object literal using square brackets [].

```
let propPrefix = "user";
let count = 1;

const dynamicObject = {
  id: 123,
  [propPrefix + "Id"]: "usr_abc", // *Key becomes "userId"*
  ["role" + count]: "admin"      // *Key becomes "role1"*
};
console.log(dynamicObject);
// *Output: { id: 123, userId: 'usr_abc', role1: 'admin' }*
```

These enhancements make object literal definitions less verbose and more flexible.

Introduction to Classes

While JavaScript's inheritance model is fundamentally based on prototypes (a more advanced topic), ES6 introduced `class` syntax as **syntactic sugar** over this existing prototype-based inheritance. Classes provide a cleaner, more familiar syntax (especially for developers coming from class-based languages like Java or C++) for creating object blueprints and managing inheritance.

A basic class definition includes:

- `class` **keyword:** Followed by the class name (typically PascalCase, e.g., MyClass).
- `constructor()` **method:** A special method for creating and initializing objects created with the class. It's called automatically when you use the new keyword.
- **Other methods:** Define the behaviors associated with objects created from the class.

```
class Product {
  // *Constructor: Initializes new Product objects*
```

```javascript
  constructor(id, name, price) {
    console.log(`Creating product ${id}...`);
    this.id = id; // *'this' refers to the new object being created*
    this.name = name;
    this.price = price;
    this.stock = 0; // *Default value*
  }

  // *Method for displaying product info*
  displayInfo() {
    console.log(`Product: ${this.name} (ID: ${this.id}), Price: $${this.price},
Stock: ${this.stock}`);
  }

  // *Method for adding stock*
  addStock(quantity) {
    if (quantity > 0) {
      this.stock += quantity;
      console.log(`Added ${quantity} stock for ${this.name}. New stock: $
{this.stock}`);
    }
  }
}

// *Create instances (objects) of the Product class using 'new'*
const laptop = new Product('P001', 'Laptop Pro', 1500);
const keyboard = new Product('P002', 'Mechanical Keyboard', 150);

// *Call methods on the instances*
laptop.addStock(10);
keyboard.addStock(25);

laptop.displayInfo();
keyboard.displayInfo();

// *Output:*
// Creating product P001...
// Creating product P002...
// Added 10 stock for Laptop Pro. New stock: 10
// Added 25 stock for Mechanical Keyboard. New stock: 25
// Product: Laptop Pro (ID: P001), Price: $1500, Stock: 10
// Product: Mechanical Keyboard (ID: P002), Price: $150, Stock: 25
```

Classes also support inheritance using the extends and super() keywords, allowing you to create specialized classes based on more general ones, but that's a topic for more advanced study. For now, understand that class syntax provides a structured way to define blueprints for objects, encapsulating their data (properties set in the constructor) and behavior (methods).

Chapter Summary

This chapter highlighted several powerful and convenient features introduced in modern JavaScript (ES6 and later) that significantly enhance the development experience. We explored **arrow functions** (=>) for their concise syntax and crucial lexical this binding. We learned about **template literals (`)** for easier string interpolation and multi-line strings. **Destructuring assignment** for arrays and objects was introduced as a clean way to extract values into variables. The versatile ... syntax was explained in its dual roles as **rest parameters** (gathering function arguments) and **spread syntax** (expanding iterables and object properties). We also covered **enhanced object literal** shorthands for properties and methods, and finally, got an introduction to the **class syntax** as a cleaner way to define object blueprints.

These modern features make JavaScript code more readable, less verbose, and often less prone to certain types of errors. As you continue your JavaScript journey, embracing these features will make your code more efficient and align it with contemporary development practices. While we've covered the core language and many modern enhancements, the JavaScript ecosystem is vast. In the next chapter, we'll briefly discuss the role of **Libraries and Frameworks** like React, Angular, and Vue, which build upon core JavaScript to provide specialized tools and structures for building complex user interfaces and applications.

19
Libraries and Frameworks

Congratulations! You've journeyed through the essential landscape of modern JavaScript. You've learned to work with variables, control program flow with conditions and loops, organize data with arrays and objects, write reusable code with functions, manage asynchronous operations like fetching data, interact with web pages via the DOM, organize code with modules, and even handle errors gracefully. With the knowledge from Chapters 1 through 18, you absolutely have the foundational skills needed to build interactive websites and web applications from the ground up.

However, as you start building more complex projects, you might notice recurring patterns or challenges. Tasks like managing the state of user interface components, handling routing between different "pages" in a single-page application, or efficiently updating the DOM in response to data changes can involve writing a significant amount of intricate code. While you *can* build everything using only the core JavaScript features we've discussed, the developer community has created powerful tools – libraries and frameworks – to streamline these common tasks, promote better code organization, and accelerate the development process. Think of it like building a house: you could build everything using only basic hand tools (core JavaScript), but using power tools or prefabricated components (libraries and frameworks) can make the job much faster and often results in a more robust structure. This chapter provides a glimpse into this "bigger picture," introducing you to the concepts of libraries and frameworks.

What are Libraries and Frameworks?

While often mentioned together, libraries and frameworks represent different approaches to leveraging reusable code.

Libraries

A **library** is essentially a collection of pre-written code (functions, classes, objects) designed to perform specific tasks. You, the developer, are in control. You decide *when* and *where* to call functions or use components provided by the library to achieve a particular result.

Imagine a specialized toolbox. If you need to tighten a bolt, you reach into the toolbox, select a wrench (the library function), and use it on the bolt (your data or task). You choose the tool for the job.

Examples of tasks libraries might help with:

- Making complex HTTP requests (though `fetch` is now quite capable).
- Manipulating dates and times (like the popular `date-fns` or legacy `Moment.js`).
- Adding animations or visual effects.
- Creating interactive charts or graphs.
- Simplifying certain DOM manipulations (like the classic `jQuery`, though less essential today with modern DOM APIs).

You integrate library code into your project and call upon its specific functions as needed to solve particular problems within your application's flow.

Frameworks

A **framework**, on the other hand, provides a more comprehensive structure or skeleton for your application. It often dictates how your application should be organized and defines the overall flow of execution. Instead of you calling the library's code whenever you want, the framework typically calls *your* code at specific points within its lifecycle. This concept is known as **Inversion of Control (IoC)** – the framework is in charge of the flow, and you plug your custom logic into designated places.

Think of a framework like a detailed house blueprint or even a prefabricated house frame. The overall structure is already defined. You don't decide where the main load-bearing walls go; you focus on filling in the details – painting the walls, installing the fixtures, adding furniture (writing your specific application logic and components) – according to the established structure. The blueprint (framework) dictates where your contributions fit.

Frameworks often provide solutions for broader aspects of application development, such as:

- **Component Model:** Defining reusable UI pieces.
- **Routing:** Managing navigation between different views or pages within the application.
- **State Management:** Handling and synchronizing application data.
- **Data Binding:** Automatically updating the UI when data changes (and vice-versa).

The key distinction: **You call library functions; a framework calls your code.** Frameworks are generally more opinionated about how you should build your application, offering a complete system, whereas libraries offer specific tools to use as you see fit.

Why Use Them?

Using libraries and, particularly, frameworks offers significant advantages, especially for larger or more complex applications:

- **Efficiency and Speed:** This is a major driver. They provide pre-built solutions for common problems, saving you countless hours of development time compared to writing everything from scratch. You don't need to reinvent routing, complex state management, or optimized DOM updates.
- **Structure and Organization:** Frameworks enforce a particular way of organizing files and code. This standardization makes projects easier to understand, navigate, and maintain, especially when working in teams. Everyone knows where to find different parts of the application logic.
- **Best Practices and Optimization:** Popular libraries and frameworks are often developed and maintained by experienced engineers. They typically incorporate optimized algorithms, performance patterns (like virtual DOM diffing for efficient UI updates), accessibility considerations, and security best practices that might be difficult or time-consuming to implement correctly yourself.
- **Abstraction:** They often hide complex lower-level details. For example, instead of manually manipulating DOM elements (Chapter 10) to update a list when data changes, a framework might allow you to simply update the under-

lying data array, and it handles the necessary DOM updates automatically through data binding.

- **Community and Ecosystem:** Widely used libraries and frameworks have vast communities. This translates to abundant tutorials, articles, courses, pre-built third-party components, extensions, dedicated developer tools, and forums where you can find help when you get stuck.

While there's a learning curve associated with any library or framework, the long-term benefits in productivity and maintainability for non-trivial projects often outweigh the initial investment.

Popular Front-End Examples

The front-end landscape (building user interfaces for web browsers) is where you'll most prominently encounter JavaScript libraries and frameworks. Their primary goal is to simplify the creation of complex, interactive, and data-driven UIs. Here are a few of the most popular players (as of the time of writing – this field evolves!):

- **React:** Developed and maintained by Meta (Facebook). Technically, React itself is a *library* focused on building user interfaces using a **component-based** approach. You create reusable UI components (like buttons, forms, cards) and compose them to build complex interfaces. It utilizes JSX, an HTML-like syntax extension for JavaScript, to define component structure. While React is a library, it forms the core of a vast ecosystem of tools and companion libraries (for routing, state management like Redux or Zustand) that together function much like a framework. It's known for its performance (using a Virtual DOM) and flexibility.

- **Angular:** Developed and maintained by Google. Angular is a comprehensive **framework** that provides an opinionated, end-to-end solution for building large-scale applications. It uses TypeScript (a superset of JavaScript that adds static typing) and includes built-in solutions for component management, routing, state management, HTTP requests, form handling, and more. Its structure is well-defined, making it suitable for large teams and enterprise applications.

- **Vue.js:** Often described as a **progressive framework**. This means you can adopt it incrementally – use it as a simple library for specific parts of a page or leverage its full capabilities for building complex single-page applications. Vue is known for its gentle learning curve, excellent documentation, and performance. It provides features like a component system, routing, and state management (Pinia/Vuex).

- **Svelte:** Takes a different approach. Instead of doing significant work in the browser at runtime (like managing a Virtual DOM), Svelte is a **compiler**. It compiles your component code into highly optimized, small, imperative vanilla JavaScript code during the build process. This can lead to very fast applications with minimal framework overhead in the browser.

Which one should you learn? There's no single right answer. It depends on the project requirements, team preferences, and job market demands in your area. The most crucial takeaway is that **mastering core JavaScript (everything covered in this book) is the essential prerequisite for effectively learning and using** *any* **of these tools.** They all rely fundamentally on the JavaScript concepts you now know.

A Glimpse at Server-Side

As we first mentioned way back in Chapter 1, JavaScript isn't confined to the browser. Thanks to the **Node.js** runtime environment, you can run JavaScript code directly on servers or your local machine.

Node.js allows developers to:

- Build **web servers** and **APIs** (like the REST APIs we learned to consume in Chapter 17). You can create the back-end logic that handles requests, interacts with databases, and sends responses back to the client (browser or mobile app).
- Create command-line tools.
- Develop real-time applications (like chat apps) using technologies like WebSockets.
- Automate build processes and development tasks (often used heavily in front-end development workflows, even if the final code runs in the browser).

Just like the front-end, the Node.js ecosystem has its own set of popular frameworks designed to simplify server-side development, such as:

- **Express.js:** A minimalist and flexible web application framework, very widely used.
- **Koa.js:** Created by the team behind Express, aiming for a more modern approach using async/await features.
- **NestJS:** A more opinionated framework (using TypeScript) for building efficient and scalable server-side applications, often drawing inspiration from Angular's structure.

The ability to use JavaScript on both the front-end (browser) and the back-end (server via Node.js) is known as **full-stack JavaScript development**, allowing developers or teams to work with a single language across the entire application stack.

This is Just the Beginning

Libraries and frameworks are powerful tools that build upon the solid foundation of JavaScript you've constructed throughout this book. They represent different philosophies and provide various levels of structure and assistance for building applications. Choosing which ones to learn and use will depend on your specific goals and projects.

Don't feel pressured to learn them all at once. The most important step you've already taken is learning JavaScript itself. That knowledge is transferable and forms the bedrock upon which all these specialized tools are built. Understanding how JavaScript works fundamentally will make learning any library or framework much easier.

Chapter Summary

In this chapter, we looked beyond core JavaScript to the broader ecosystem of tools designed to make development more efficient and scalable. We clarified the distinction between **libraries** (toolboxes you call upon) and **frameworks** (blueprints that call your code), highlighting the concept of Inversion of Control in frameworks. We discussed the key benefits of using these tools, including improved efficiency, structure, adherence to best practices, and leveraging community support. We briefly introduced some of the most popular **front-end** options like **React**, **Angular**, and **Vue**, emphasizing their role in building user interfaces. We also revisited **Node.js** as the platform enabling JavaScript on the **server-side**, allowing for full-stack development. We stressed that mastering core JavaScript is the essential foundation required before diving deep into any specific library or framework.

You've now seen the core language, how it interacts with the browser, how it handles asynchronous tasks, how to organize it, and the landscape of tools built upon it. You have a comprehensive map of the JavaScript world. The final step in this initial journey is to solidify your understanding and gain confidence through practice. In the next, and final, chapter, we'll discuss practical next steps, suggest project ideas, point you towards valuable resources, and encourage you on your continued learning path.

20

Next Steps

You have reached the end of this particular path through the world of modern JavaScript. From the initial "What is JavaScript?" in Chapter 1 to understanding the landscape of libraries and frameworks in Chapter 19, you've covered a vast amount of ground. The goal of this book was to provide a step-by-step guide for beginners, building your knowledge layer by layer. Now, equipped with these foundational concepts, you stand ready to truly start building, experimenting, and deepening your expertise. This final chapter isn't an end, but rather a signpost pointing towards the exciting roads that lie ahead in your ongoing programming journey.

Recap: What You've Learned

Take a moment to reflect on the journey. You began by meeting JavaScript (Chapter 1) and understanding its role. You then mastered the fundamental building blocks: variables, data types, comments (Chapter 2), and the operators needed to manipulate them (Chapter 3). You learned to control the flow of your programs with conditional statements (Chapter 4) and automate repetition with loops (Chapter 5).

Next, you tackled organizing data, first with ordered lists using Arrays (Chapter 6) and then with structured key-value pairs using Objects (Chapter 7). You discovered the power of reusable code blocks through Functions (Chapter 8) and demystified the crucial concepts of Scope and Hoisting (Chapter 9).

With the core language covered, you moved into the browser environment, learning to interact with web pages through the Document Object Model (DOM) (Chapter 10) and respond to user interactions with Events (Chapter 11). You then confronted the world of asynchronous programming, understanding Callbacks (Chapter 12), the improved structure of Promises (Chapter 13), and the clean syntax of `async/await` (Chapter 14). You learned to handle the unexpected gracefully with Error Handling techniques (Chapter 15) and to organize your growing codebase using Modules (Chapter 16).

You ventured into communicating with servers by working with APIs and the `fetch` command (Chapter 17), explored convenient modern JavaScript features like arrow functions and destructuring (Chapter 18), and finally got an overview of the wider ecosystem of Libraries and Frameworks (Chapter 19).

You've built a comprehensive understanding of modern JavaScript fundamentals.

Practice, Practice, Practice!

Reading about programming concepts is one thing; truly internalizing them requires **active coding**. Knowledge solidifies when you apply it to solve problems and build things. The more you code, the more fluent you'll become, and the more intuitive these concepts will feel. Don't be afraid to experiment, make mistakes, and learn from them – that's a natural and essential part of the process.

Here are a few ideas for projects you can tackle using the skills you've acquired. Start simple and gradually increase complexity:

- **Interactive To-Do List:** This is a classic beginner project for a reason. You'll practice DOM manipulation (adding, removing, marking items as complete), event handling (button clicks, maybe input field changes), and perhaps even storing the list data temporarily (though persistent storage is a further step).
- **Simple Quiz Game:** Create a multiple-choice quiz. You'll need to structure your questions (perhaps using arrays of objects), handle user selections (radio buttons or buttons), check answers, keep score, and display results – all involving DOM manipulation and event handling.
- **Weather App (using a public API):** Find a free weather API online. Use `fetch` (Chapter 17) to get weather data for a city entered by the user. You'll practice asynchronous JavaScript, handling JSON responses, and updating the DOM to display the fetched information (temperature, conditions, etc.). Error handling for failed API requests is also important here.

- **Basic Image Carousel/Slider:** Create a simple image viewer with "Next" and "Previous" buttons. This involves managing an array of image sources, handling button clicks, and updating the `src` attribute of an `<img>` tag.
- **Tip Calculator:** A straightforward application involving input fields for the bill amount and desired tip percentage, a button to calculate, and displaying the tip amount and total bill. This reinforces handling user input, basic calculations, and updating the DOM.

Choose a project that interests you, break it down into small, manageable steps, and start coding. Don't aim for perfection initially; aim for making it work, then refactor and improve.

Essential Resources

As you continue learning and building, you'll inevitably encounter questions or need to look up specific details. Knowing where to find reliable information is crucial.

- **MDN Web Docs (Mozilla Developer Network):** This should be your primary resource. Maintained by Mozilla and the community, MDN provides comprehensive, accurate, and up-to-date documentation on JavaScript, HTML, CSS, Web APIs, and more. It includes detailed explanations, interactive examples, and browser compatibility information. Make MDN your first stop when looking up language features or browser APIs.
- **Online Developer Communities:** Platforms like Stack Overflow, Dev.to, and others host vast communities where developers ask and answer questions. Searching these sites (using specific error messages or keywords) can often provide solutions to problems others have already faced. Remember to search thoroughly before asking a new question, and when asking, provide clear, concise code examples and describe the issue accurately. Reading how others solve problems is also a great way to learn.
- **JavaScript Specification (ECMAScript):** For the truly deep dive, the official ECMAScript specification defines the language itself. It's highly technical and dense, not typically beginner reading, but it's the ultimate source of truth for language behavior.

Effective searching is a skill in itself. Learn to formulate specific search queries using keywords, error messages, and the concepts involved.

Keep Learning: Advanced Topics

The topics covered in this book form the foundation, but the world of JavaScript is vast. As you gain confidence, here are some areas you might explore next:

- **Deeper Dive into Functions:** Closures, higher-order functions, functional programming patterns (`map`, `filter`, `reduce`).
- **Object-Oriented Programming:** Prototypes, inheritance patterns, advanced class features.
- **Asynchronous Patterns:** Advanced Promise usage, generators, async iterators.
- **Testing:** Writing automated tests (unit tests, integration tests) using frameworks like Jest, Mocha, or Vitest to ensure your code works correctly.
- **Build Tools & Development Workflow:** Tools like Vite, Webpack, Parcel, and package managers like npm or yarn, which automate tasks like bundling modules, transpiling modern code for older browsers, and managing project dependencies.
- **TypeScript:** A popular superset of JavaScript that adds static typing, helping catch errors during development, especially in larger projects.
- **Framework Deep Dives:** Choose one of the frameworks mentioned in Chapter 19 (React, Vue, Angular, Svelte) and dedicate time to learning its specific concepts and ecosystem.
- **Node.js Development:** Explore server-side JavaScript, building APIs, interacting with databases, and understanding the Node.js environment.
- **Web Performance & Optimization:** Techniques for making your web applications load faster and run more smoothly.
- **Web Security:** Understanding common vulnerabilities (like XSS, CSRF) and how to write secure code.

Don't feel overwhelmed by this list! Pick areas that interest you or are relevant to the projects you want to build, and learn them incrementally.

Chapter Summary

This concluding chapter served as a reflection on the knowledge you've gained throughout this book, summarizing the key milestones from basic syntax to asynchronous programming and modules. The critical importance of **practice** was emphasized, along with concrete **project ideas** to help solidify your skills. We highlighted essential **resources**, particularly **MDN Web Docs**, for continued learning and reference. We also provided a glimpse into more **advanced topics** you might explore as your journey continues. Programming, especially with a dynamic language like JavaScript in an ever-evolving ecosystem, is a journey of continuous learning.

www.ingramcontent.com/pod-product-compliance
Lightning Source LLC
LaVergne TN
LVHW081341050326
832903LV00024B/1257